New Every
Morning

LEAH SLAWSON

New Every
Morning

*Devotions
Celebrating God's
Faithfulness*

BARBOUR
PUBLISHING

Published by Barbour Publishing, Inc., 1810 Barbour Drive, Uhrichsville, Ohio 44683, www.barbourbooks.com

Our mission is to inspire the world with the life-changing message of the Bible.

Member of the
Evangelical Christian
Publishers Association

Printed in the United States of America.

Contents

Introduction

*Thou art worthy, O Lord, to receive glory and
honor and power: for thou hast created all things,
and for thy pleasure they are and were created.*
REVELATION 4:11 KJV

With the dawn of every new day, the undeserved grace of God awaits us. Through the created world and the body of Christ, God provides hourly for every physical and spiritual need we have. His protecting angels guard us when we close our eyes in sleep. Our God, who created us for His pleasure, is faithful to us in every way. What a cause for celebration!

Late have I loved you, O Beauty ever ancient, ever new, late have I loved you! You were within me, but I was outside, and it was there that I searched for you. In my unloveliness I plunged into the lovely things, which you created. You were with me, but I was not with you. Created things kept me from you; yet if they had not been in you they would have not been at all. You called, you shouted, and you broke through my deafness. You flashed, you shone, and you dispelled my blindness. You breathed your fragrance on me; I drew in breath and now I pant for you. I have tasted you, now I hunger and thirst for more. You touched me, and I burned for your peace.

—St. Augustine

His Divine Presence

Misplaced Faith

*Put not your trust in princes, in a son of man, in whom
there is no salvation. When his breath departs, he
returns to the earth; on that very day his plans perish.*
PSALM 146:3–4 ESV

Sometimes it seems the entire world is connected—
through texting, phone calls, tweets, status updates,
blogging, and the list goes on. We all want to communicate with one another—all the time. We want
to speak and have an audience, and we want to
read and listen to what others say. We need and
depend on one another, and that's not necessarily
a bad thing. We were created for interdependence
like parts of a body. But it's easy to cross that line
of trusting in people more than trusting God, talking
to friends more than talking to Jesus, seeking
counsel rather than seeking the Counselor.

Our tendency is to find someone who can help us,

who will say what we want to hear, and who will answer back in 140 characters or less. Our instantaneous connection with others carries with it the danger of putting all our trust and hope in others. We put faith in our companies, our political parties, our social groups, our teachers, even our preachers. We can always find another blog to read, website to peruse, sermon on podcast, text to respond to, or email to read. We become dependent on these relationships, and before we know it they have displaced faith. Our time and our thoughts are consumed with the words of everyone but God. Scripture tells us people are here and gone in the blink of an eye. In a moment, our plans perish with us.

Only Jesus—only His presence is lasting in our lives. Only He will be with us in this world and the next, every moment of every hour.

---

*I praise You, Father, for Your lasting
presence in my life. Thank You for
being the author and finisher of my faith.*

God's Invitation

Who is the man who fears the LORD? Him will he instruct in the way that he should choose. His soul shall abide in well-being, and his offspring shall inherit the land. The friendship of the LORD is for those who fear him, and he makes known to them his covenant.

PSALM 25:12–14 ESV

The old adage "You can choose your friends, but you can't choose your family" might bring to mind a challenging family relationship—maybe you stuck by relatives in tough times or when they were difficult to get along with. But stop and think about the choice aspect of friendship. One of the reasons we value a good friendship so much is because it is a relationship of choice. We can walk away. We can find someone else to talk to or share our experiences and secrets with. In a good friendship, there is reciprocity. Each brings something to the relationship that is valuable to the other.

Now think about what it means to be offered the friendship of God. He is choosing to be in a relationship with you. He wants what is good for you. He wants to give to you. He desires your time, your stories, and your experiences. He wants to know you, to hear what is on your mind, to have you depend on Him, to seek His counsel. He is not hiding or being evasive but rather longs to reveal more and more of Himself to you. Celebrate God's invitation of friendship to you. Thank Him for keeping your soul safe.

Father, Thank You for the privilege of being Your friend.

God Listens

*But truly God has listened; he has
attended to the voice of my prayer.*
PSALM 66:19 ESV

So few of us are truly good listeners. Listening takes time. Listening is an act of love. Listening involves eye contact, feedback, and sympathetic responses. Sometimes listening well means exercising incredible self-control. It is easier to talk, to tell another how to fix her problem, than it is to sit and listen while she figures it out for herself. Listening to a small child or an elderly person can be tiresome and irritating when we're in a hurry. Listening is exercising patience.

Listening is an act of humility. It's letting someone else have center stage and burying your ego's need to be seen or in control of the conversation. Listening makes you vulnerable—you never know what news you're about to receive, what secrets you may be asked to keep.

God is a true and right listener. He attends. Every word, every sigh, every scream, every thought that bubbles up in your mind is heard by God. His ears and His eyes are always turned to His children's voices.

Praise Him today for His undivided attention, for listening constantly to the inhale and exhale of your breathing, the beating of your heart, the most secret thoughts of your mind.

Praise You, Lord, for listening to me.
Help me by Your spirit to listen well to others.

Carry the Cross

Bear one another's burdens,
and so fulfill the law of Christ.
GALATIANS 6:2 ESV

The Christian life is not meant to be solitary. We are part of a body, all connected, and we need one another. When we get overwhelmed, someone else will pray for us, listen to us, encourage us, or provide for us. We, in turn, are called to help others. This is a way of being Christlike. Jesus carried His cross up Calvary for us. He lived, suffered, died, and rose again for us. In response to Him, what can we do for someone else? How can we help carry a burden?

We usually think of the physical things we do first—visit the sick, take food to those in need, or run errands. These are all good and needed. But how can we carry spiritual burdens? Listen attentively to a friend when she needs to sort out her problems. Pray in secret when she comes to your mind. Fast for someone. Pray aloud with a friend. Give her encouragement by the sound of your voice lifting her name to God. Ask God what you are called to do and for whom? Then listen as He tells you how to carry the cross for another. Celebrate the faithfulness of God in providing friends who help you.

Father, bring to my mind the friends who need my prayers today. Thank You for those who help and encourage me in my journey. Give me opportunities to encourage others.

Perfect Friendship

Now that we have actually received this amazing friendship with God, we are no longer content to simply say it in plodding prose. We sing and shout our praises to God through Jesus, the Messiah!
ROMANS 5:11 MSG

Some ideas can't be captured in ordinary language. They demand the rhythmic and figurative language of poetry and song. Love, honor, freedom, heartache, celebration, perseverance, courage, and friendship: thousands of poems and songs pay tribute to these ideals. We have been given the highest form of friendship, the most complete friendship, and an unfailing, never disappointing friendship. God has chosen to be in a relationship with us. He has called us His friends.

Even the best of friends, the most loyal and constant person, can disappoint or desert us. No one can be the perfect friend all the time. We can't imagine friendship except in the human terms we have experienced. Yet what God extends to us is even higher and better than the best human friend we've known. He is right here, all the time, closer than a phone call, quicker than a text message. He is immediate and ever present. Through the Holy Spirit, we have constant access to God; we are never without His comfort, wisdom, joy, counsel, strength, and discernment.

Praise to You, Father, for always being ready to listen, counsel, comfort, and strengthen me.

Knowing Him

The LORD is faithful in all his
words and kind in all his works.
PSALM 145:13 ESV

When you meet new people, how do you get to know them? You talk, you listen, and in the give-and-take of conversation you discover who they are. You do things together—either work or play—and you see how they respond to the good and the bad of life. Who is she in crisis or under stress? Who is he in times of celebration? Over time, you learn their character and motivations. You can see if they don't do as they say.

Words and work. What we say and what we do reveal who we are. One without the other is incomplete, but together they reveal our character. What is true of us is even more so with God. Throughout history, God has been faithful to speak through His prophets, the written scriptures, and His risen Son. We can hear His words, and we can see His actions. But are we trying to have a relationship with Him?

God has faithfully given us the means to know Him. Do we set aside time to talk to Him? Do we note His ongoing work in our daily lives and the lives of our friends and family? His kind works and faithful words are there for us to see, to hear, to know, and to trust—if only we will look.

Father, thank You for making Yourself known to me. Stir in me the desire to know You more deeply.

Rest in God

*For a day in your courts is better than a
thousand elsewhere. I would rather be a
doorkeeper in the house of my God than
dwell in the tents of wickedness.*

<small>PSALM 84:10 ESV</small>

Nearness. Think about the nourishing satisfaction of spending time in the presence of someone you love and who loves you. A parent, a child, a spouse, a sister, an old friend—their company can bring joy when we take time to be with them. How much more can we be satisfied by the presence of God. In moments with Him, we find deep rest. We can relax as we release our cares in prayer. We can be cleansed, healed, and restored when we are in His presence.

Though it is fun (and sometimes therapeutic) to have a girls' night out, go to a spa, chat with a friend on the phone, or do some retail therapy, ultimately those are temporary symptom relievers. We can't heal our deepest hurts, ease our stresses and worries, or forgive grudges by trying to escape them. Real change takes place when we still ourselves in God's presence, sometimes even in wordless prayer, and trust His presence to do the work that only He can do. Seek Him. Go to His doorstep. Put yourself in places where His presence can most easily be experienced—a sanctuary, a quiet place outside, in scripture. James 4:8 (ESV) says, "Draw near to God, and he will draw near to you." Thanks be to God for the promise of His presence, for inviting us to dwell with Him.

Father, help me to draw near to You.
Restore me in the stillness of Your presence.

Spirit's Intercession

Meanwhile, the moment we get tired in the waiting, God's Spirit is right alongside helping us along. If we don't know how or what to pray, it doesn't matter. He does our praying in and for us, making prayer out of our wordless sighs, our aching groans. He knows us far better than we know ourselves, knows our pregnant condition, and keeps us present before God. That's why we can be so sure that every detail in our lives of love for God is worked into something good.

Romans 8:26–28 MSG

Language is essential to humanity. What we cannot name with words doesn't exist for us. It is virtually impossible to think of something that can't be spoken in language. One of our most frustrating experiences is to be at a loss for words. Yet we find ourselves without words at times. Facing tragedy, deep wounds, confusion, or complex problems, we simply do not know what to say or how to pray at times.

Praise God that we don't have to know. We don't even have to speak. He has given us the Holy Spirit, who prays with us and for us. When we can only sigh or weep, the Spirit translates that to prayer. When we moan in pain, the Spirit carries it as prayer to the throne of heaven.

When scripture tells us we have everything we need for life and godliness, it means everything. We have a continual intercessor praying for us what we cannot pray ourselves.

Thank You, Father, for providing the Holy Spirit, who constantly interprets my prayers and hears me even when I can't find the words to express myself. You know what is wrong in my heart before I even find the words to name it.

Crying to God

O LORD, God of my salvation;
I cry out day and night before you.
PSALM 88:1 ESV

If you've ever been in a car or on an airplane with a crying infant, you know how nerve-grating continual crying can be. No matter how compassionate you may feel for the baby or the mother, the ear-piercing screaming is hard to tolerate for very long. Even a patient and loving parent will try anything to stop the crying.

As humans, we can't fully understand the patience of our heavenly Father. In our best moments, even toward those we love, we cannot endure continual crying. Yet God never loses patience. He continually hears us with love and compassion, desiring our highest good and acting accordingly on our behalf. He doesn't give in to our demands, unless it's for our good. He has no limit to how much or how often we can cry to Him. Rather, He delights in hearing us and helping us. He comforts us with a patience and compassion and presence far beyond the most loving earthly parent. Do not hesitate to cry out to God. Do not try to "be a big girl." He knows your heart, and He knows your hurt. He never tires of hearing from you.

---

*Praise and thanks to You, Father God,
for always being attuned to my cry.*

*S*alvation is from our side a choice;
from the divine side it is a seizing upon,
an apprehending, a conquest by the Most
High God. Our "accepting" and "willing"
are reactions rather than actions. The right of
determination must always remain with God.

—A. W. TOZER

His Saving Grace

Only Jesus

*Jesus looked hard at them and said, "No chance
at all if you think you can pull it off yourself.
Every chance in the world if you trust God to do it."*

MATTHEW 19:26 MSG

Jesus looked hard at his disciples. The context of that
verse is the rich young ruler, the man who wanted
to earn his eternal life. He had jumped through the
hoops, so he thought. He was a law keeper. When
Jesus restated the commandments to him, he said
he had kept every one, so Jesus probes further. He
tells the man to sell all he has and give it to the poor.
At that point, the young man turns away.

The problem was not his possessions, per se. The
problem was his desire to earn his way into God's
kingdom. He had done such a good job keeping
all the law. The wealth he had was a gift from God,
but he didn't see it that way. He saw it as his own

to control and maintain. This is why Jesus targeted him with that specific question. The disciples, who witnessed this scene, were confused. They wanted to know who has a chance of obtaining eternal life. That is what earns them a hard look from Jesus. Grace is standing in front of them. Grace has been teaching them daily, and they still don't get it. Their only chance is His very person.

Trust God. God the Father made a way through the Son, Jesus Christ. That's it. The only chance, the only hope, the only thing worth clinging to in this life and for the next is Jesus.

Lord Jesus Christ, cause me to remember
daily that You are my only hope.

Receive the Word

So what exactly was Moses saying? "The word that saves is right here, as near as the tongue in your mouth, as close as the heart in your chest." It's the word of faith that welcomes God to go to work and set things right for us. This is the core of our preaching. Say the welcoming word to God—"Jesus is my Master"—embracing, body and soul, God's work of doing in us what he did in raising Jesus from the dead. That's it. You're not "doing" anything; you're simply calling out to God, trusting him to do it for you.
ROMANS 10:8–10 MSG

"Will you marry me?" "You've got the job." "It's a deal; your house finally sold."—these are powerful words to the ones receiving them. Just a few words, written or spoken, can alter the direction of your life.

The most important word, the most life-changing word ever spoken, is the Word of God Himself—the

Son, Jesus Christ. Scripture tells us He is the Word, the very mind of God, made incarnate to live and die in our place so that we might be reconciled to our heavenly Father and restored to continual fellowship with the triune God. God did all the work. He sent His Word to us. We only have to welcome that Word into our lives by saying yes to Him.

Enable me, Lord Christ, to welcome
You every moment into my life.

Captured by God

*And Mary said, "My soul magnifies the Lord,
and my spirit rejoices in God my Savior, for he
has looked on the humble estate of his servant.
For behold, from now on all generations will call
me blessed; for he who is mighty has done great
things for me, and holy is his name."*

Luke 1:46–49 ESV

When Mary arrived to visit her cousin Elizabeth, the
baby (John the Baptist) in her womb leaped for joy
at the sound of Mary's voice. Elizabeth greets Mary
with the words, "'Blessed is she who believed that
there would be a fulfillment of what was spoken to
her from the Lord'" (Luke 1:45 ESV). Mary takes no
credit for her own faith but launches into the song
of praise known as The Magnificat. In doing so, she
exemplifies the response of a soul captured by God.

"'My spirit rejoices in God my Savior,'" she says

(Luke 1:47 ESV). Mary knows her need. We rejoice in a savior only if we see ourselves as lost, dependent, and in need of protection. Mary is jubilant because Almighty God has regarded her. His attention is on her. He has chosen her. She is humble, aware of her status as His handmaiden, mindful that He could have chosen anyone else, and honored to be given the privilege of bearing His Son to the world. She knows that her name will now be known to all generations, but not because of her great deeds, rather because the Mighty One has done great things for her. Mary is the picture of one who has received Christ—humbled, honored, and full of praise.

---

*Empty me of myself, O Lord, so that I
may be filled with the life of Your Son.
Make me like Mary, rejoicing in my Savior.*

Finding What Wasn't Sought

Isaiah dared to speak out these words of God: People found and welcomed me who never so much as looked for me. And I found and welcomed people who had never even asked about me.

ROMANS 10:20 MSG

Finding something exciting when you are not looking for it is a delightful experience. What fun it is to stumble on a great sale while shopping. . .and everything you try on fits perfectly. Or even better, running into an old friend you've lost contact with. And how many people have fallen in love just when they had given up, or gotten a great job offer when they weren't even looking for new employment? It is a wonderful surprise to find something fulfilling that you were not even seeking.

This is how it is with God. We are dead in our trespasses and sin. We have no idea what we really need or even want in our lives, and then He shows up and opens our eyes and our hearts to His great love for us in Jesus. When we come to know Him, we wonder how we ever thought we could live our lives without His presence. We weren't even looking for the one thing we most wanted and needed; but knowing that about us, He pursues us in love and draws us to Him.

Thank You, Lord Jesus, for saving me when I was not looking for You and opening my eyes to Your presence in my life.

Peter and Judas

The One who died for us—who was raised to life for us!—is in the presence of God at this very moment sticking up for us. Do you think anyone is going to be able to drive a wedge between us and Christ's love for us?

ROMANS 8:32 MSG

Jesus washed the feet of Peter and Judas. Peter denied Him, and Judas betrayed Him. But Jesus served and loved them both.

We are both Peter and Judas. We are prone to deny our identity with Jesus and betray our friends and our beliefs. Sin dwells in us, and despite our best efforts, we disappoint others and ourselves continually. Failure in relationships and failure to live up to our own standards are so common to our human experience that we tend to forget there is another reality—Jesus. Christ, the Son of God, the incarnate Savior, died in our place and was raised to eternal life for us. He is forever at the right hand of God pleading for us. He cannot deny us, and He will never betray us. Such love is beyond our human ability to grasp; yet He gives us glimpses of it. And our hope rests on the truth of His love.

Nothing can separate us from His love—because of His character, not our actions. Thanks be to God for His faithfulness to us despite our daily denials of Him in our lives.

Father, I am grateful that Your forgiveness extends to the Peter and the Judas in me. Thank You for mercifully beginning again with me each day.

Saving Grace

For You have delivered my soul from death.
Have You not kept my feet from falling, that I
may walk before God in the light of the living?

PSALM 56:13 NKJV

The saving grace of God through Christ Jesus is a daily and ongoing work in our lives. Though we may well remember a moment when we decided to follow Christ, His work in us had begun before that, so our hearts would be open to Him. We rejoice that we are saved from eternal apart from God and that we have a hope for life after death, but our salvation is not just for the life beyond the grave. It is here and now. The psalmist makes it plain. Yes, our souls are delivered from death, but our feet are also kept from falling here and now. In this physical and material world, God is guiding our feet, making plain our paths, and protecting us from sin, temptation, and evil in the world around us.

We have no idea what is around the next corner, in the next hour; but God knows. He knows and He sends His angels to protect us and be with us. "For He shall give His angels charge over you, to keep you in all your ways" (Psalm 91:11 NKJV).

Rarely do we go to bed at night thinking about the possible "near misses" of the day. Yet, if we could see into the heavenly realm, we might be surprised at how many times each day God's saving power is at work to keep us walking in His light.

Father, I praise You for Your saving work,
for keeping me—mind, soul, and body—
every hour of every day.

Transforming Presence

Then Levi held a great banquet for Jesus at his house, and a large crowd of tax collectors and others were eating with them. But the Pharisees and the teachers of the law who belonged to their sect complained to his disciples, "Why do you eat and drink with tax collectors and sinners?" Jesus answered them, "It is not the healthy who need a doctor, but the sick. I have not come to call the righteous, but sinners to repentance."

LUKE 5:29–32 NIV

The invitation of Jesus is an invitation to a changed life. He does not invite us to a religious system or a set of rules. He does not invite us to be a particular kind of person or belong to a certain group. He invites us to life with Him, being changed both inside and out.

We often try to clean up our own acts or to

change our behavior by our own wills. We not only fail at this, but we also end up blindly living by rules and adding our own to the Gospel of grace. Jesus' offer is to have Him with us. . .in whatever shape we are in at the moment. His presence will do the work that our lives need. The Pharisees and teachers of the law of His day heavily criticized Him. The most religious among His culture disapproved of His companions, yet that was precisely why Jesus came: to bring transforming grace to those who needed Him.

Thank You, Lord, for coming into my life,
for being willing to dine with me,
for coming to save sinners.

Lose to Gain

"Simply put, if you're not willing to take what is dearest to you, whether plans or people, and kiss it good-bye, you can't be my disciple."
LUKE 14:33 MSG

To be a follower is to be a student. Students cannot learn from a teacher they don't trust. The students trust the teacher to show them what they don't know or take them where they have not been. The students must also lay aside any previous false assumptions in order to move forward in their thinking. Without trust, the students won't do what is necessary to progress in what they claim they want to learn.

Jesus told his followers that to be His disciples, they must be willing to give up the things most precious to them. The willingness to let go of what is dearest to us, whether a relationship, a dream, or a possession we treasure is an act of trust. This is why Jesus asked such a hard thing. To make it plain that being a disciple is based on trust. Plans, people, possessions—none of those are bad things, and often we are not required to forsake them; but Jesus is interested in the heart. Does the heart trust Him enough to let go? Does the heart know that Jesus, the embodiment of love, will fill it back up with good things? Is the heart willing to be emptied so Jesus Himself can fill it?

Thank You, Father, for saving grace in Jesus Christ. Thank You for being trustworthy. Give me a heart willing to let go of whatever is in the way of following You.

*I*t is only when men begin to
worship that they begin to grow.
—CALVIN COOLIDGE

His Transforming
Power

A Pilgrim's Life

Blessed are those whose strength is in you,
whose hearts are set on pilgrimage.
PSALM 84:5 NIV

Blessed means "happy." Happy is the one whose strength is in God—not herself. Happy is the woman who is not operating on the strength of her own skill, talents, and experience, but rather is relying on God, aware of her dependence and pushed beyond her own capabilities. Happy is the woman who is open to newness and taking risks. This may sound more like a definition of stress than of happiness and seem more nerve-racking than peaceful. Not depending on yourself is counter-intuitive. It's un-American. The ego will constantly resist relying on God for strength. Yet the psalmist is clear that happiness is found when we look to God and not ourselves.

This same verse says happy is one whose heart is set on pilgrimage—a journey for spiritual significance. Happy is the woman who is searching for God, searching for the unseen world, looking for the eternal in the everyday, desiring the presence of God, longing to see and experience the work of the Holy Spirit. Pilgrimage by definition is a moving, evolving, changing state. When you're traveling, the scenery constantly changes. The pilgrim life is one of change, of moving forward, and of forgetting what lies behind. A life of movement and change may also seem contrary to what we think happiness is, since we often spend our time and energy protecting what we have and preserving things as they are. Yet, God's Word assures us that trusting Him with our lives and searching for Him daily is where our real satisfaction is found.

Thank You, God, for faithfully drawing me to Yourself, for putting it in my heart to seek You and depend on You. Give me a pilgrim's heart for You.

Rehearsing God's Goodness

Once again I'll go over what GOD has done,
lay out on the table the ancient wonders;
I'll ponder all the things you've accomplished,
and give a long, loving look at your acts.
PSALM 77:11–12 MSG

Rehearsals. Musicians, dancers, actors, and speakers all know the necessity of rehearsing. The actress memorizing lines for a play goes over them again and again. The pianist plays the scales repeatedly. Athletes call it practice, but it's the same thing. Drill after drill ensures that execution in the game will be flawless. Students go over material repeatedly if they are studying for a test. Reviewing is an essential part of learning.

As human beings, we cannot live without reminders, without repeating or rehearsing things that are important for us to know. One way to care for our souls, to put ourselves in a position to receive grace and draw near to God, is to go over His deeds. Ponder God's work in your life. Take a long look. Remember. Remind yourself. Keep a journal if you like to write things down. Look back at old pictures that carry you to a different era of your life. Pause and think about all you have come through since then. Read the scripture and recount God's deeds throughout history.

Don't expect yourself to stay faithful. You won't, and you can't in your own strength. Make a habit of rehearsing God's goodness, reminding yourself what He has done for you and others you know. Remember, and you will be encouraged.

Thank You, Father, for the gift of memory.
Help me to remember Your faithfulness and to
rehearse Your good deeds toward Your people.

Favorite Word

We thank you, God, we thank you—
your Name is our favorite word;
your mighty works are all we talk about.

PSALM 75:1 MSG

The classic movie *The Sound of Music* contains a wonderful song about favorite things. From cream-colored ponies to schnitzel with noodles, the song-writer suggests that thinking of your favorite things can change the way you feel. The truth of that song resonates with us. A favorite color painted on the walls of a room or hanging in our closet makes us happy. The car radio surprises us with our favorite song on the way to work one rainy Monday morning. A friend sends a bouquet of our favorite flowers for a birthday gift. All these bring smiles to our lips. Almost everyone can rattle off her favorite movie or book. Favorites have power. We've chosen them because they mean something to us, bring out something in us, and change the way we feel.

It's not so typical to have a favorite word. Few of us have thought about our favorite words. Yet the psalmist says God's name is his favorite word. What a suggestion. Think of the power in the name of Jesus. Scripture says one day every knee will bow at the sound of His name. When you're afraid, call on your heavenly Father who protects you. Call Jesus' name when you are lonely, and experience the presence of the closest Friend. When you need guidance, the Counselor is the one to call. "Wonderful Counselor, Mighty God, Everlasting Father, Prince of Peace" (Isaiah 9:6 NIV). Think of all the names of God that can become our favorite words—to bring out the best in us, to change the way we feel.

Holy God, Wonderful Counselor, Prince of Peace, thank You for all Your many names. May they become my favorite words.

Fear of Change

*Later, a great many people from the Gerasene
countryside got together and asked Jesus to leave—
too much change, too fast, and they were scared.
So Jesus got back in the boat and set off.*
LUKE 8:37 MSG

The phrase "asked Jesus to leave" in Luke 8 is a little startling. How could anyone do such a thing? It's easy to hastily judge the people from the Gerasene countryside. Who on earth would ask Jesus to leave?

But if we look closer, we can identify with their reasons—"too much change, too fast, and they were scared." Haven't we all felt that way? Leaving home, beginning college or a job, a new marriage, a baby, the death of a loved one, a divorce, a disease, the empty nest, facing old age. Life is nothing if not an ongoing series of changes, moving quickly, sometimes several at once. What woman is not afraid?

How do you react when those changes come—cry out to Jesus, run to His presence, do everything possible to put yourself in a place to receive grace? Or hold tight with a clenched fist to what you know? Hunker down and get through it? What about the changes that come as a result of being Christ's follower? Do you embrace or resist the presence of Christ changing your life?

It is easier than you might think to "ask Jesus to leave." When you resist His presence, His invitation, His communion, you are, in essence, asking Him to go away. Thank Him that He is faithful to love us and to stay with us even in those times that we push Him away.

Lord Jesus Christ, thank You for Your presence in my life, even when I try to push You away. You will see me through every change in life. Help me to trust You.

Perspective on Troubles

*We continue to shout our praise even when
we're hemmed in with troubles, because we know
how troubles can develop passionate patience in us,
and how that patience in turn forges the tempered
steel of virtue, keeping us alert for whatever God
will do next. In alert expectancy such as this,
we're never left feeling shortchanged.*

ROMANS 5:3–5 MSG

Shouting God's praise when we're in trouble doesn't come naturally. It's not usually our first reaction when we're boxed in, worried, or facing a crisis. Yet scripture tells us we can and should shout God's praises, even in the worst of situations.

How does that work?

Troubles develop patience. Time keeps moving. Events unfold. Circumstances take shape. Waiting for problems to get solved, watching healing slowly take place, and seeing a crisis move through its stages demand that we slow down, observe, and afterward, that we reflect. Moving through this cycle brings about patience in us.

Patience leads to virtue. What does that look like? Our reaction time increases; we think before we speak because we've learned from our last trouble. We become more Christlike because we are more temperate, grateful, reflective, deliberate women. As our character changes, our perspective shifts. We now look at trouble in a different way: We look for God's work in our lives. Character change brings a new point of view. We see with new eyes; we see more of God. Then we aren't left feeling shortchanged. And seeing Him is worth shouting about!

Thank You, Lord, that You are working in my life, transforming my character and changing my perspective through the troubles that come my way. Grant me patient endurance and more faith in You.

The Spirit Can

Those who think they can do it on their own end up obsessed with measuring their own moral muscle but never get around to exercising it in real life. Those who trust God's action in them find that God's Spirit is in them—living and breathing God! Obsession with self in these matters is a dead end; attention to God leads us out into the open, into a spacious, free life. Focusing on the self is the opposite of focusing on God. Anyone completely absorbed in self ignores God, ends up thinking more about self than God. That person ignores who God is and what he is doing. And God isn't pleased at being ignored.

ROMANS 8:5–8 MSG

God is faithful to empower us to live the life He calls us to. He has given us the Holy Spirit, dwelling in us to do what we can't do alone. Our problem is that we forget what we've got. We forget that indwelling power of the Spirit. We can't resist impulsiveness, temptations, and compulsions, but the Spirit can. We cannot love our enemies and do good deeds to those who are spiteful to us, but the Spirit can. We cannot forgive and forget, but the Spirit will. We cannot put others ahead of ourselves, but the Spirit does. We cannot love perfectly those who need our love, but the Spirit will.

All we can do--in fact, all we need to do is admit our need. We must face our own emptiness and weakness and trust God to do the impossible for us. He has saved us. He has given us the Spirit's presence. We have "everything we need for life and godliness," and our only work is to trust His already completed work. When we trust, we discover God's Spirit at work in our hearts, doing daily for us what we could never do for ourselves.

Celebrate God's faithfulness in sanctification. As Philippians 1:6 (NIV) says, "He who began a good work in you will carry it on to completion."

Father in heaven, thank You for giving me the transformative power of the Holy Spirit.

Faithful and True

Now may the God of peace himself sanctify you completely, and may your whole spirit and soul and body be kept blameless at the coming of our Lord Jesus Christ. He who calls you is faithful; he will surely do it.

1 THESSALONIANS 5:23–24 ESV

Personal transformation sounds easy according to book and magazine covers. Everything can be done in easy steps or a certain number of weeks. Articles and books provide deceptively simple formulas for changing our lives. The problem, and the reason there is no end to this type of writing, is that transformation, real and lasting change, comes from a deeper place. Real change happens in the heart, and it comes from a force beyond us.

God promises to sanctify us, to keep our spirits, souls, and bodies blameless. The presence of the

Holy Spirit in our daily lives works to change us. We cannot see the change happening. We might be going through a difficult relationship, a crisis at work, or a physical struggle, but in it He is at work shaping us to be more Christlike, changing our perspective, and showing us His love for us. He calls us to this transformed life, and He will ensure that it happens. When John penned his vision, he described Jesus this way: "Now I saw heaven opened, and behold, a white horse. And He who sat on him was called Faithful and True" (Revelation 19:11 NKJV).

Faithful and True are the names of the One who called us to a blameless life. Celebrate that He will accomplish it.

Transformation is Your work, O God,
and not mine. Give me eyes to see and
faith to believe and strength to persevere.

His Work

Just think—you don't need a thing, you've got it all! All God's gifts are right in front of you as you wait expectantly for our Master Jesus to arrive on the scene for the Finale. And not only that, but God himself is right alongside to keep you steady and on track until things are all wrapped up by Jesus. God, who got you started in this spiritual adventure, shares with us the life of his Son and our Master Jesus. He will never give up on you. Never forget that.

1 Corinthians 1:7–9 MSG

Life often seems chaotic and frenzied, out of control and moving too fast. Steady and on track are not words today's woman would use to describe her life. The media offers us continual suggestions for how to improve certain areas of our lives, leaving us feeling like we never measure up and that we just aren't doing enough. We need a new habit, a better product, a deeper relationship, a get-away weekend, a girls' night out—a constant barrage of suggestions comes our way constantly to convince us that our lives are not what they are supposed to be. We need to try harder, do better, and regroup.

But God's Word offers us hope right where we are. He has given us all we need to travel the road He has put us on. He has a final destination for us, and it is not in this world. He started the life we have, which He calls an adventure, and through Jesus He has equipped us for everything we will face along the way. His Word says He will never give up on us. He initiated our lives. This is His work. He isn't depending on us for our sanctification, rather He gives us the power to grow and change, and He is moving us toward the final result: eternity with Him.

Thank You, Lord Jesus, for leaving me Your Holy Spirit to enable me to live and grow in You. Make me mindful of Your constant grace and work in my life.

Good from Bad

"Now here's a surprise: The master praised the crooked manager! And why? Because he knew how to look after himself. Streetwise people are smarter in this regard than law-abiding citizens. They are on constant alert, looking for angles, surviving by their wits. I want you to be smart in the same way—but for what is right—using every adversity to stimulate you to creative survival, to concentrate your attention on the bare essentials, so you'll live, really live, and not complacently just get by on good behavior."

LUKE 16:8–9 MSG

Jesus tells an unusual parable of an unscrupulous manager who is losing his job. The man uses his wits, his resources, his past experiences, and his contacts to figure out how to survive and is then praised by his boss for his shrewdness. The trial in his life brings out the best in the man.

Jesus illustrates the need for his followers to do the same: use attention, wisdom, experience, and even adversity for what is right. He has equipped us with everything we need. We have talents, skills, experiences, relationships—all of which can be drawn upon to do what is right, to follow Christ's path for us, to further the Gospel and to transform us.

Difficulties and misfortunes, even tragedies, do not have to make us bitter. By the Spirit's power, these times can burn away the things in our lives that are depleting us or keeping us from fully experiencing Christ in us. They can help us pay closer attention to what matters, to draw us nearer to Christ and to others. "It was good for me to be afflicted so that I might learn your decrees" (Psalm 119:71 NIV).

Father, I offer gratitude for every life experience, good and bad. Help me know how to use them all for Your glory and Your good.

*I*f then, you are looking for the way by
which you should go, take Christ,
because He Himself is the way.
—THOMAS AQUINAS

His Call to Follow

Grace Abounding

And God is able to bless you abundantly,
so that in all things at all times, having all that
you need, you will abound in every good work.
2 CORINTHIANS 9:8 NIV

Discouragement creeps in easily when we are tired or stressed. When circumstances are not to our liking, we tend to complain or turn inward with anger or depression. So often, without even being aware, we are thinking that life is all up to us and we can't get people to do what we want or events to turn out like we have planned. What is wrong? We have forgotten the words of Paul in this short verse.

God is able. Ability, power, and resources are all His. He can do anything.

God is gracious. He is a giver of more than we deserve: forgiveness, strength, time, talents, and blessings both tangible and intangible.

He is able to be gracious in all things at all times. No exceptions. In any area of your life, God can work however and whenever He chooses. Anytime He wants to show up and change things, He can and He will.

Your needs are covered. If you think you have a need that God is not covering, discuss it—with Him. Ask Him, "Lord, do I think I need this and I really don't?" Ask Him to open your eyes to see His perspective on what you need.

Look for God's grace abounding in what you do. Scripture says you will abound in every good work. What areas of your life do you feel like you are failing in? What places are you not measuring up?

Father, show me what Your good works for me are. Help me to trust You to make me abound in them.

Calling of Jesus

Then Jesus addressed them, "Let me ask you something: What kind of action suits the Sabbath best? Doing good or doing evil? Helping people or leaving them helpless?" He looked around, looked each one in the eye. He said to the man, "Hold out your hand." He held it out—it was as good as new! They were beside themselves with anger, and started plotting how they might get even with him.

LUKE 6:9–11 MSG

Read the Gospels. Follow Jesus from town to town and watch what He does. Look at where He goes and with whom He associates. He deliberately challenges the Pharisees by healing this man's hand on the Sabbath right before their eyes. He looks them in the eye just before He does it. He has a point to make.

Life in Christ, moving as His Spirit directs, will

sometimes bring criticism. Some people will not understand the choices you make, the places you go, and the people you help. When your life begins to resemble Christ's, your critics will resemble His. People who live for others' approval or a group identity, who follow the rules to fit into the system, will not always understand the call you hear and may resent your freedom in Christ and react to it, just as the Pharisees reacted to Jesus.

Celebrate the calling of Jesus in your life and the freedom you have in Christ Jesus. Seek to follow Him in engaging the culture and helping those in need. Ask Him where to go and what to do; then turn a deaf ear to the modern-day Pharisees.

Thank You, Christ Jesus, for calling me to Your kingdom. Close my ears to the critics, and open them to Your direction for my life.

Work It Out

Hate evil and love good,
then work it out in the public square.

AMOS 5:15 MSG

Amos's words are short and succinct, but a lifetime of learning is in these words. Notice that before we "work it out in the public square," the prophet says to "hate evil and love good." How does one do that? A good start is to pray the words of Psalm 51:10 (ESV): "Create in me a clean heart, O God, and renew a right spirit within me." Our natural bent is self-serving. Our own preservation, comfort, or ambition is where our hearts will lead us without the cleansing power of the Gospel at work in our lives, so begin with praying for a clean heart, one that hates evil and loves good. This is a prayer God will answer. He desires that we love what He loves and hate what He hates. This is the beginning of becoming more like Christ.

As He changes our desires, our likes and our dislikes, and He purifies our hearts, we begin to see the Gospel being worked out in our own public square. Selling dresses? Trying cases? Teaching school? Caring for the sick? What does hating evil and loving good look like in our workplaces? God is faithful to show us the answer. He has chosen the paths we travel, given us the work we do—God wants our work lives to bear witness of Him. Our Christian lives are not a Sunday thing but a constant fragrance of the Gospel being spread hourly wherever we are.

Thank You, Father God, for Your faithfulness
to shape me into the likeness of Your Son
and to use me in the spread of His kingdom.

Ready for the Call

*Blessed be the LORD my Rock, who trains
my hands for war, and my fingers for battle.*
PSALM 144:1 NKJV

David as a young boy was put in charge of his father's flocks. He trained his eyes and his hands on those hillsides, protecting helpless sheep from predators with his slingshot. When the time came to step up and slay Goliath, the young David had muscle memory in his hands and accuracy in his eyes like no man in Saul's army. Later David's path led him to Saul's courts, his friendship with Jonathan, and eventually to be king of Israel. Step-by-step, year by year, God was preparing David in the present for the calling of his future.

He does no less for each of us. Some are schooled in music or art; others, in athletics. Some of us are effective communicators, trained to speak or write; or you might be a problem solver, accurate in analysis. Whatever God's call, He prepares his people through His sovereign guidance of our lives. Life's experiences prepare us for the moments when we step into the battle for the kingdom of God.

Reflect today on how God has readied your hands, your eyes, your mind, and your heart for the calling you have.

Thank You, Father in heaven, for Your faithful provision in my life, which has always prepared me for the next step You direct.

Passing the Gift

Through Him we received both the generous gift of his life and the urgent task of passing it on to others who receive it by entering into obedient trust in Jesus. You are who you are through this gift and call of Jesus Christ!

ROMANS 1:5–6 MSG

God the Father, through His Son, Jesus Christ, faithfully gives to us His very life by the power of the Holy Spirit. This gift is cause for celebration. We have everything we need for this life and the next. Jesus saves us from the grip and destruction of sin daily and has promised us eternity.

He has also given us purposeful and meaningful work, to pass on the life of grace to others who will receive it. We don't do this in our own power or through our own agenda. Rather, we simply share the gift we have been given. Our lives are marked by both honor and humility—honor, that such treasure would choose to descend and dwell in us; humility, because we bring nothing in exchange for His great gift. Live today in celebration of the gift of eternal life and grace you have received. Live today passing that gift to others.

Thank You, Lord Jesus Christ, for the gift of grace. Enable me to share it with others through the work You have given me to do.

Valuable Work

Now we command you, brothers, in the name of our Lord Jesus Christ, that you keep away from any brother who is walking in idleness and not in accord with the tradition that you received from us. For you yourselves know how you ought to imitate us, because we were not idle when we were with you, nor did we eat anyone's bread without paying for it, but with toil and labor we worked night and day, that we might not be a burden to any of you. It was not because we do not have that right, but to give you in ourselves an example to imitate.

2 THESSALONIANS 3:6–9 ESV

The world doesn't value work. Many people try to avoid it or get it over with quickly. A live-for-the-weekend mentality pervades our culture. Some only value certain kinds of work. Work only matters if it pays well or carries prestige. But work is a gift of

God. He values work. He did it for six days in creation. Work is part of our being made in His image. We each have a vocational calling. Whether the work is managerial or menial is irrelevant. God values it all. He shows no favorites and is not a respecter of persons. Your diligence in your work, your attention to your work, and your pleasure in your work all matter to God. They all are opportunities to bring glory to Him and fulfillment to you as you flourish where He has placed you.

Jesus' work on the cross on our behalf means that God is always pleased with us. He sees us clothed in Christ's righteousness. God is pleased with our work because He designed it for us, provided it for us, and equipped us to do it. Consider your attitude about work. Thank God for providing pleasure in work, for a calling that gives purpose to your daily tasks.

---

*Father, help me to be grateful for the
work You have given me to do,
to see it as Your gift to me.*

God's Presence

Now the word of the LORD came to Jonah the son of Amittai, saying, "Arise, go to Nineveh, that great city, and call out against it, for their evil has come up before me." But Jonah rose to flee to Tarshish from the presence of the LORD. He went down to Joppa and found a ship going to Tarshish. So he paid the fare and went down into it, to go with them to Tarshish, away from the presence of the LORD.

JONAH 1:1–3 ESV

Twice, the phrase "from the presence of the Lord" appears in this one verse. You can't miss it. Notice who is doing the moving—not God, but Jonah. Though God was present with Jonah, Jonah was unaware of it while he was on the run from God.

No matter how satisfying we think a place or an experience may be, it is impossible to be satisfied outside of His presence. That is the "not quite" feeling we get, the something that is missing, the gnawing feeling of discontent when we think we should be happy with all we have or with being where we thought we wanted to be.

Noise and busyness can drown out God's call. We can ignore God's pull for a long time and pretend that we are not missing His presence. But stillness and silence won't lie. Pause. Be still, and in the silence ask, "What is my 'Tarshish'? What call do I not want to follow?" Turn back in repentance. Surrender again to God.

God's call includes God's presence. No matter how difficult the call, the place, and the tasks, He is with us, comforting us, enabling us, satisfying us, and meeting our needs.

Thank You, gracious God, for the
call and for the continual grace
to repent and return to You.

Simple Call

*The man whom he had delivered from the demons
asked to go with him, but he sent him back, saying,
"Go home and tell everything God did in you."
So he went back and preached all over town
everything Jesus had done in him.*
LUKE 8:38–39 MSG

The man delivered from demons, in profound gratitude, wanted to follow Jesus, literally. He asked to accompany Him, but Jesus sent him home. Jesus had delivered him from bondage to freedom; He had given the man his life back, and this man's response was natural: to give his life to Jesus by going with Him. Jesus had a claim on his life, and He had a calling for the man; but it was not to go with Him literally. Rather, Jesus told the man to go home and tell people about everything God had done for him.

Sometimes things are too simple and uncomplicated for us to believe that they are true. All Jesus wanted from this man was for him to return to his own home. Do the same job, see the same people, go to the same village events—same life—but different. Return home and live as the new, free man Jesus had made him to be. Live in peace when once he had raged. Live in stillness when once he had been a maniac. When people marveled at the change in the man, he was to tell them what God had done in him. Simple. He wasn't called to deliver sermons on Sunday, write a book, or debate apologetics. He wasn't required to know all the theological answers. His call—live his life at home and tell everything God had done for him.

Celebrate God's saving, delivering work in your life today. Celebrate the simplicity of your calling, then go and tell.

Thank You, Lord Jesus, for the simplicity of Your call. Strengthen me to go and tell what You have done for me.

Call to Humility

"When you're invited to dinner, go and sit at the last place. Then when the host comes he may very well say, 'Friend, come up to the front.' That will give the dinner guests something to talk about! What I'm saying is, If you walk around with your nose in the air, you're going to end up flat on your face. But if you're content to be simply yourself, you will become more than yourself."

LUKE 14:10–11 MSG

God doesn't want His people to be anything other than exactly who we are. He plans to make His strength perfect in our weakness. He intends to be glorified in our humility. He doesn't call us to try to be more than we are by our own strength. He calls us to acceptance—acceptance of ourselves as needy, dependent, flawed human beings and acceptance of Him as our only hope to produce anything good.

God works through us when we are not seeking our own gain. When we have our noses in the air, we can't see the world around us—the needs of others, the opportunities to serve, or the stumbling blocks at our own feet. We are blinded by pride, and the fall is soon to come.

When Jesus tells us to go and sit at the last place, He is giving us a physical reminder of His way in the world. Take the road of humility, as He did. Listen for His Spirit's direction, as He listened to His Father's.

Father, by Your enabling Spirit may
I practice the humility of Christ.

*I*f God sends us on strong paths,
we are provided strong shoes.

—CORRIE TEN BOOM

His Provision

Notice His Gifts

*You cause the grass to grow for the livestock
and plants for man to cultivate, that he may
bring forth food from the earth and wine to
gladden the heart of man, oil to make his face
shine and bread to strengthen man's heart.*

PSALM 104:14–15 ESV

Oxygen, water, corn, wheat, cattle, eggs, grapes, medicines, warmth. . .there is no end to the physical provisions of God that we can see and touch and count when we pause to do so. Everything we need has been created and put on earth for our use. In addition to those tangible things, God has provided us with abilities to make money, skills to communicate, the capacity for kindness and compassion, the will to survive, and the desire to be needed and to serve others.

Every good thing, those we can touch and

those we can't, are gifts from God. How often do we recognize the most basic things in life as being God's gifts?

What do we have that is ours? Our money—but how did we earn it? A talent—where did it come from? An education—how about the opportunity, capacity, and energy to achieve? Our family—who planned our births? Health—can you really control it? We are children, provided for by a Father. Everything belongs to God. Take time to notice.

Father in heaven, help me to see
the smallest of things before my
eyes that are Your gifts for me.

God the Source

*"Sovereign LORD, you have made the heavens
and the earth by your great power and
outstretched arm. Nothing is too hard for you."*
JEREMIAH 32:17 NIV

What woman doesn't need more creativity, more energy, and more strength to endure the long haul? While building a career, maintaining a marriage, rearing children, taking care of elderly parents, or dealing with old age or grief, women are constantly facing new challenges, situations that test their strength and push their endurance to new limits, and problems that demand new ways of thinking and creative solutions. The psalmist offers us a simple prayer that turns our attention God-ward and reminds us of the truth.

God is the sovereign Lord of the universe. He has made the heavens, the earth, and everything in them by His own power, strength, and creativity. He is the very source of those things. If He can do that, if He is power, strength, and creativity, then has He not provided them for us when He made us to be His own? Second Peter 1:3 says that He has given us everything we need for life and godliness.

Our problem is that we can't remember. We experience a lack of creativity, strength, or power and are overcome by the problems in front of us. But we forget to ask the very Source who offers Himself to us freely. Have a problem to solve? Take it to the One who lights the galaxies. Need strength? Pray to the One who suspended the planets in space. Praise God today that He is the source of everything. Memorize this simple verse, and make it a daily prayer.

God, help me to remember that You
are the source of everything I need.
Nothing is too hard for You.

Live near the Stream

"Blessed is the man who trusts in the LORD, whose trust is the LORD. He is like a tree planted by water, that sends out its roots by the stream, and does not fear when heat comes, for its leaves remain green, and is not anxious in the year of drought, for it does not cease to bear fruit."

JEREMIAH 17:7–8 ESV

A tree planted by a river or lake is a healthy tree. A constant water source is near to nourish it through its roots. It stays green in a dry year when other trees, farther away, may wither and die. A tree in distress doesn't produce fruit and is more likely to suffer damage when strong winds come.

The tree by the water represents the person who trusts in God. When a woman draws near to God, when the Living Water is a constant presence in her life, she is productive, strong, prepared, and able to provide for others. A well-watered, growing tree provides a home to animals and shade to people. A woman who draws her nourishment from Jesus daily will be ready and able to give her life to others; she can continue to be productive and strong despite difficult circumstances around her. She does not fall prey to anxiety because she lives close to the stream--the Living Water, Jesus Christ.

Thank You, Lord Jesus, that You are the Living Water, that I never have to thirst because You have given Yourself to me.

Armed for Battle

Finally, be strong in the Lord and in the strength of his might. Put on the whole armor of God, that you may be able to stand against the schemes of the devil.
EPHESIANS 6:10–11 ESV

No matter how peaceful a people, history teaches that wars happen and a nation must be prepared to defend her people. From fortifying cities with walls and wearing steel or bronze armor to developing smart bombs and nuclear weaponry, we have always found ways to prepare against attack and be ready when an enemy comes. For many Americans, September 11, 2001, seemed to come out of nowhere, a surprise attack for which we were unprepared. Thousands of civilians were unarmed when they lost their lives that day.

In the spiritual battles in our lives, we are not unarmed and we are not fighting as one individual against the enemy. We fight as one of God's own, surrounded by an army of saints. The battle is His, and He has equipped us, dressed us in His armor and provided for our protection. We have every piece we need. His armor is tested and can withstand any onslaught; and the final outcome, no matter who wins today's skirmish, is already determined.

Go into your day in confidence, remembering whose armor you wear.

---

*Father God, cause me to remember
my armor—helmet, shield, sword, belt,
breastplate—that You have provided.
Give me confidence in You for today's battles.*

Falling into God

The LORD upholds all who are falling
and raises up all who are bowed down.
PSALM 145:14 ESV

Today's women juggle many roles at once. Our culture is busier than ever, and we seem to take on more roles than are humanly possible. Many of our modern conveniences have led us to believe we have more time, so we should be able to get more done. Technology allows us to multitask, and though we brag about our ability to do it, it's unhealthy for our minds and spirits. At some point, every woman hits a wall. One of the plates she is spinning falls. With no margins for error in life, if something goes wrong or needs extra attention, then something else doesn't get done—and stress piles up. She might feel frantic, hit the panic button, or maybe even experience anxiety attacks.

So how do you end this cycle? Stop. It seems counterintuitive if you think you are short on time, but do it anyway. Be still. Pet the dog, or make a cup of tea. Go outside if the weather is nice, or sit by the fireplace. Play some music. Breathe deeply. Unfold your hands and tell the Lord that you are letting go. Relinquish control of your life. He will catch you. No matter how many years you have known Him, you might still need this reminder. Our nature is to continually try to manage ourselves in our own strength. Just turn back again to the Lord. He is reaching for those who are falling and upholding those who are stumbling beneath their burdens.

---

*Thank You, Lord, that Your arms
are always outstretched to catch me.
Help me to remember to seek You in stillness.*

Reach for Jesus

*Jesus said to her, "Daughter, you took a risk of faith,
and now you're healed and whole. Live well,
live blessed! Be healed of your plague."*

MARK 5:34 MSG

A woman who had been bleeding for twelve years struggled through the crowds to find Jesus. She believed that if she could touch Him, just brush His clothes, that the divine life in His body could heal her. When she finally got close enough and reached out to Him, He was aware of her. His disciples thought Him crazy when he asked, "Who touched Me?" Yet He perceived in that touch her need of Him, and the energy to heal her flowed from His body. The power was His, not hers. Healing is His choice, not ours; but she did what she could do to put herself in a place where she could be touched by Jesus.

What places can we go to be touched by Jesus?

What things do we press through to get to Him? Being still and silent, praying, reading scripture, sharing with others, being honest about what we want and need from God—all of these put us in a place where Jesus can meet us and heal us. Like the woman in the story, we only have to reach toward Him desiring to be made whole.

I want to reach for You, Lord Jesus, not the things of the world. Heal my broken places, and make me whole.

Step into Risk

But if you see that the job is too big for you,
that it's something only God can do, and you trust
him to do it—you could never do it for yourself
no matter how hard and long you worked—well,
that trusting-him-to-do-it is what gets you set
right with God, by God. Sheer gift.

ROMANS 4:4–5 MSG

Trusting God. . .it's easier said than done. By definition, trusting God means you're not trusting yourself. You have checked everything off your list. Your own resources are spent. You're out of ideas. You're tired and overworked. You have reached the end of yourself. You feel helpless. This is a good place to begin: at the end of yourself.

To trust God is to step into risks, to take on what seems impossible, to embrace what is larger than your known capacity. It is to untie the boat from its moorings, even if storm clouds are brewing. It is to be planted out on a craggy cliff rather than live potted in a greenhouse. It is to grow from between the cracks in the sidewalk.

God is faithful. Jesus is the evidence that He will do all. He will pay in full. He will meet every need. Trusting Him moment by moment is our only part. Think about the places in your life where you are operating in your own strength and becoming exhausted. Are there areas where you rely only on your own resources? Are you looking at the odds rather than to your heavenly Father? Let go of doing it all on your own, and trust God instead.

Heavenly Father, I fear letting go. Help me to surrender my agenda and trust You for strength for what lies ahead.

Christ Within

*I pray that out of his glorious riches he may
strengthen you with power through his Spirit
in your inner being, so that Christ may
dwell in your hearts through faith.*

Ephesians 3:16–17 niv

Inner strength. It's something we all hope we'll have when we need it. Problems and crises are inevitable. We know trouble will come; it's just a matter of when. We don't have to live in fear and dread though. Scripture teaches that we have inner power through the Holy Spirit. He is working in us, even when we are unaware, to enlarge Christ's life in us. Our faith is growing even when we cannot see it. The Holy Spirit is working in us so that we are able to do God's will for our lives; otherwise we would never choose the right way on our own. Our inner self can be strong because the source of the strength is not from within us but from the God of the universe. There is no end to His riches, from which this power comes.

Meditate on what it means to have Christ living in you. Christ reacts to your coworkers. Christ loves that difficult family member perfectly. Christ serves the neighbor in need. Christ is patient during sickness. Christ is quiet when falsely accused.

We don't call on our own strength, will, or ideas; rather, we call on the Christ who lives in us by God's Spirit. Paul prayed this for all who would read his letters. Let us pray this for others and ourselves.

Father in heaven, thank You for the power of Christ living in me. Help me to remember this as I move through my day.

God's Attention

"Has anyone by fussing before the mirror ever gotten taller by so much as an inch? If fussing can't even do that, why fuss at all? Walk into the fields and look at the wildflowers. They don't fuss with their appearance—but have you ever seen color and design quite like it? The ten best-dressed men and women in the country look shabby alongside them. If God gives such attention to the wildflowers, most of them never even seen, don't you think he'll attend to you, take pride in you, do his best for you?"

LUKE 12:25 MSG

Think about the idea of God attending to you, taking pride in you, doing His best for you. Hasn't He done so for all of His creation? Look at the infinite variety and beauty of the physical world. Notice how every creature has food, drink, and a habitat suited to its needs. The lizard matches the green of the grass;

the squirrel, the gray of the tree bark. Polar bears have white fur and plenty of blubber. Hound dogs track scents, and herding dogs move sheep. Fish, crustaceans, and sponges have the coral reefs. Tall pines are homes to owls, and gnarly oaks house hives for bees.

When we pause to reflect on the detail and precision with which God designs and cares for His world, it isn't logical that we would worry about ourselves. Yet we do. We fuss over our appearance, our homes, our children, our bank accounts, and our health. We worry about our hairstyles and our paint colors, our kids' birthday parties and the chemicals in our food supply. We spend time, energy, and money on the temporal things of life, while saying that the eternal is what matters to us. Perhaps the antidote is to walk outside. Look around at the beauty of the fall leaves. Breathe in the fresh clean air after a spring rain. Remember that God attends to you, takes pride in you, the crown of His creation, and does His best for you.

Thank You, Lord of heaven,
for always having Your loving eye on me.

*T*here is not a square inch in the whole domain
of our human existence over which Christ,
who is Sovereign over all, does not cry, "Mine!"
—ABRAHAM KUYPER

His Sovereignty

A Whole Heart

Teach me your way, O LORD, that I may walk
in your truth; unite my heart to fear your name.
PSALM 86:11 ESV

The psalmist knows that there is a divine plan, an order to his life, an ordained path that he should walk, and help available to do it. In walking that path, his life will bring honor to God. What a great prayer to remind us that God has a purpose for our lives. We often forget that there is a way for us marked out by God. We need only to pray that we will see and know it. God is always leading us, if only we will heed His direction.

We walk the path of truth. We seek to live in the freedom of truth, to be honest in word and deed, and to proclaim what we know to be true. This is what it means to walk in the truth.

How can we do this? It takes a united heart. The

psalmist knew his heart was divided, and we are born with divided hearts as well. It's why we both love and hate, control and indulge, are generous and stingy, encouraging and critical.

A whole heart is a reverent one directed toward heaven. It is a heart turned God-ward in thinking and feeling. You can't do this through your own will. It is a spiritual grace. Pray for a unified heart. Only He can bring you wholeness of heart.

Father, teach me to pray the words of the psalmist, that my life might reflect Your truth and Your wholeness and bring honor to Your name.

Accepting

*They started arguing over which of them
would be most famous. When Jesus realized
how much this mattered to them, he brought a
child to his side. "Whoever accepts this child as
if the child were me, accepts me," he said. "And
whoever accepts me, accepts the One who sent
me. You become great by accepting, not asserting.
Your spirit, not your size, makes the difference."*
LUKE 9:46–48 MSG

Imagine how disheartening, even frustrating, it
must have been for Jesus to listen to his followers
argue over being great or famous. Concerning His
kingdom, they had it so wrong. Yet in His gentle way,
He pulled to Himself a small child to illustrate what
He wanted them to learn.

Adults accept children as children; they don't
hold them to the same standards as adults. They

don't set the same expectations for them or try to place them in categories or label them. Who greets a child with "What do you do for a living?" or "Where are you from?" In Jesus' day, a child would have been "the least of these" in society—last in line, last to be listened to or be respected. Yet Jesus was likening accepting Him to accepting the very least one. The one who takes in that small, insignificant child, who matters least to the world around him, is the heart ready to receive Jesus. This heart is a humble and trusting one, not one jockeying for position or networking for status.

To trust Christ is to accept the smallest things, the least significant positions, without thought of how the world will measure it. Jesus said, "You become great by accepting, not asserting." Personal empires, social status, political stature—power and control—are not what matter. But accepting the child of Bethlehem's manger and whatever He brings into our lives is most important.

Create in me a willing heart, Father,
to accept whatever You bring my way
in life's journey. Thank You for leading me.

Ponder the Power

Woe to you who turn justice to vinegar and stomp righteousness into the mud. Do you realize where you are? You're in a cosmos star-flung with constellations by God, a world God wakes up each morning and puts to bed each night. God dips water from the ocean and gives the land a drink. GOD, God-revealed, does all this. And he can destroy it as easily as make it. He can turn this vast wonder into total waste.

AMOS 5:7–9 MSG

Morning and night. Sunshine and rain. Turning leaves, blowing wind, crashing waves all evidence the powerful cycles at work in the universe. Observe the animals as they hunt their prey and care for their young. Sun, water, and dirt produce food to fuel them day after day. Look at the fish or the egg on your plate, which gives you energy for the day ahead. Your life depends on a balance of nutrients stored in them. Everywhere we turn we see the cycles of nature, the power of the universe at work, the energy moving from one thing to the next, keeping it all in balance. Every created thing is interdependent.

God's mind, His majestic power and control, are behind it all. Imagine if it were to stop. We worry about other people, other political parties, or other countries. We worry about day-to-day circumstances with our families, our jobs, our health, or our friends. What is any of this compared to the awesome power of Creator God? Pause and contemplate that power. What if the tides stopped, the sun did not set, the rain did not fall? He can command those things to stop as easily as He once said, "Let there be. . ." Just a few minutes of meditation on the wonder of all that is and how it works (what little we understand of it) brings us back to our knees in worship. Ask God for a moment of a big-picture view.

Almighty God, cause me to pause and ponder how powerful You are. Thank You for sustaining all of life every day.

Keeping Watch

Behold, the eye of the LORD is on those
who fear him, on those who hope in his
steadfast love, that he may deliver their soul
from death and keep them alive in famine.
PSALM 33:18–19 ESV

Keeping watch. There is great comfort in knowing someone is keeping watch. Whether it is our military over the nation or our police force over our community, we need to know someone is alert to danger and watching over us when we are vulnerable. We watch our small children constantly, knowing their foolishness and ignorance of the dangers around them. We sit with a sick loved one in the hospital, listening to his every breath and the constant beeping of the monitors.

This is God's image mirrored on the earth. Picture Almighty God doing the same for you. He is watching all your surroundings while you travel or while you sleep. He sees you working, you walking out of the grocery store, and you cooking dinner. He watches you at play, and He listens to every breath you take, whether you are sick or well. He is watching when you laugh, and He hears you when you cry.

Thank God for His constant eye on you. You are never out of His sight.

Father of heaven and earth, keep me mindful of Your constant guard over my life. Thank You for taking care of me.

Jesus Leads

*Calling the crowd to join his disciples,
he said, "Anyone who intends to come
with me has to let me lead. You're not in the
driver's seat; I am. Don't run from suffering;
embrace it. Follow me and I'll show you how."*

MARK 8:34 MSG

Jesus does not ask us to go live for Him and call Him for help only when we need it—though that is how life often works. No. His call for us is to follow Him. He leads. He drives. We watch and go where He goes. Picture a child, following behind a parent, stepping where he steps, turning where he turns. Jesus specifically tells us not to run from suffering, yet our prayer lists are often full of just that. . . alleviate the pain, remove the trial, fix the problem.

Jesus' invitation includes suffering, but in the suffering there is another option that the world doesn't have—to do it like He did—for the Father's glory and for the kingdom's sake. This is redemptive suffering. Pain is inevitable, but it can also be purposeful. We can only experience purpose, even if we can't understand it, if we are following Jesus. He is choosing the route our lives take. We are stepping where He steps and turning where He turns and trusting Him for everything on our paths.

Thank You, Lord Jesus,
for encountering first
everything I will ever face.

Fear Subdued

*He is my steadfast love and my fortress, my stronghold
and my deliverer, my shield and he in whom I take
refuge, who subdues peoples under me.*

PSALM 144:2 ESV

Fear is a part of every woman's life at some point, if
not a constant for many. A little girl is afraid of the
dark or afraid of going to a new school. A grown
woman is also afraid of the dark—the unknown
future—and afraid of the new, because new always
involves change.

Be it college, marriage, a job, childbirth, mother-
ing, empty nesting, old age, or death, there is
always change and the unknown around the next
bend of life. In all those stages too are people we
interact with. Often fear of other people becomes
a problem, even an idol. We let others and their
opinions intimidate us and have power over us. Fear

robs us of the freedom that Christ has given us.

God is faithful to prepare us for the next step in our lives, to lead us through dark places, and to come to our aid when we want to cower in the face of intimidation. Through Christ, every force that causes fear has been subdued. Nothing has authority in our lives except God. Rehearse His love in your life. Remember times of kindness and protection.

Think about when He has been your fortress and subdued those who sought to do you harm. When you remember Him this way, your fears begin to subside.

Lord Christ, thank You that You
have power over everything that
I fear. Help me to trust You more.

God's Leading Hand

God is kind, but he's not soft.
In kindness he takes us firmly by the
hand and leads us into a radical life-change.
ROMANS 2:4 MSG

A mother sees her preschooler arguing with a playmate. Tempers escalate, as small jaws are set and skin flares red. What does she do? Almost universally, mothers intervene in a scene like this. They walk over and take their own child firmly by the hand, separating him from the soon-to-be destructive situation. This act is not anger but kindness. This is a mother who loves a child enough to rescue him, to show him a better way, even when he doesn't want to be, or think he needs to be, rescued.

God's love for us encompasses all the best of a mother and father's love. He created both the guidance and protection of a father and the gentleness and nurturing of a mother. He loves us even more than our earthly parents love us—and more than we love or will love our own children. His love is not rooted in His need for us, because He is complete and secure within Himself. But it is strong enough to take us firmly by the hand and lead us to change. Pray for a sense of God taking you by the hand and a willingness to surrender to change.

---

*Father God, thank You for loving me
enough to lead me firmly. Make me aware
of Your guidance and willing to follow You.*

Embrace Expectancy

This resurrection life you received from God is not a timid, grave-tending life. It's adventurously expectant, greeting God with a childlike "What's next, Papa?" God's Spirit touches our spirits and confirms who we really are. We know who he is, and we know who we are: Father and children. And we know we are going to get what's coming to us—an unbelievable inheritance! We go through exactly what Christ goes through. If we go through the hard times with him, then we're certainly going to go through the good times with him!

ROMANS 8:15–17 MSG

Remember being a child. Think of the excitement of Christmas morning or an upcoming birthday party, the anticipation of a family trip or a special meal, the eagerness to go new places, learn new things, or make new friends. You had no part of planning or responsibility for these events; you just enjoyed them. Youth is a time of expectancy. We want to grow up, to get to the next stage of life, whether it is wearing makeup, driving a car, going to college, getting married, or having children. Life itself feels like an adventure.

The new life we receive in Christ gives us the capacity to live our entire lives feeling this way—adventurously expectant. God is our Father; we are His children. Nothing in our future will come as a surprise. He is eternal. He has already been there and lived the next moment, year, or decade. Because of that, we can wake up every day with a "What's next?" attitude. The future is not unknown to the Father; it is only unknown to us as children. God is fully aware of every friendship we make, every trip we take, every job we do, every problem we face. Embrace expectancy, thanking God that He's faithfully sovereign over your future.

Almighty God, You know every step and turn of my life. Give me faith to trust You for the adventure that lies ahead.

Celebrate God's Protection

Jesus said, "I know. I saw Satan fall, a bolt of lightning out of the sky. See what I've given you? Safe passage as you walk on snakes and scorpions, and protection from every assault of the Enemy. No one can put a hand on you. All the same, the great triumph is not in your authority over evil, but in God's authority over you and presence with you. Not what you do for God but what God does for you—that's the agenda for rejoicing."
LUKE 10:18–20 MSG

Suppose a man fought off an intruder trying to enter his home or property. That would be a great feat to be proud of. Yet no one would want to have to do it every night. Most people go to sleep at night with the comfort that a police force is on duty in their area. And 911 is only a phone call away. Someone is in charge of protection, in authority, wide awake and watching while the rest of the city rests.

Jesus has given us authority over evil. Because we belong to Him, we have authority over the forces of evil. And He tells us there is even greater cause to celebrate. The real triumph is God's authority and presence over us. While we go about our daily lives, God is reigning over all creation. No events surprise Him. Nothing happens that He doesn't foresee. He is ever-present in our lives, guarding and guiding us even when we are completely unaware of His work.

Just as we sleep peacefully night after night, never giving thought to those protecting our streets and our neighborhoods, we often go through our days oblivious to the presence and protection God has all around us. Jesus says this is the truth we should really celebrate.

Thank You, Lord, for Your continuous watchful care over my life. Forgive me for all the times I forget Your presence with me.

Hanging on His Words

*And he was teaching daily in the temple.
The chief priests and the scribes and the principal
men of the people were seeking to destroy him,
but they did not find anything they could do,
for all the people were hanging on his words.*
LUKE 19:47–48 ESV

A patient waits for a doctor to come in and give her results from tests or surgery. Her ear is fine-tuned to every word he is going to speak. A young couple who are falling in love pay rapt attention to each other's words, trying to read the nuance, innuendo, and inflection in each word, which might move the relationship to the next level. Sitting at the bedside of a dying friend, a loved one leans in, straining to hear what may be the very last words that person speaks. All of these are times when we hang on every word another says.

Consider the power of Jesus' words. Though the Pharisees were trying to trap Him, the people around Him hung on every word He said. Jesus spoke the world into being. He spoke to water, wind, and waves. All creation responds to the sound of His voice. He is the Word of God in human form.

We have in the Gospels the recorded words of Jesus during His life here on earth. How important are those words to us? Do we read them over and over? Do we allow them a life-giving place in our lives? Are we like those who came to hear Him speak—hanging on His every word?

Lord Jesus, create in me the
desire to cling to Your every word.
Give me ears to hear when You speak.

I have been all things unholy. If God can work through me, He can work through anyone.

—ST. FRANCIS OF ASSISI

His Deliverance

Free from Fear

"I'm speaking to you as dear friends. Don't be bluffed into silence or insincerity by the threats of religious bullies. True, they can kill you, but then what can they do? There's nothing they can do to your soul, your core being. Save your fear for God, who holds your entire life—body and soul—in his hands."

LUKE 12:4-5 MSG

The Pharisees of Jesus' day were looking for any excuse to trap Him in His own words. They listened intently and questioned Him at every turn to try to catch Him violating religious law. They were an intimidating presence to the disciples, no doubt, and Jesus knew this. Thus, He warned them about caving in to the pressure.

When we're outnumbered by the crowd usually we either keep our mouths shut or feign agreement. All too often these are our default positions. Silence or insincerity—Jesus warned His disciples against both. To choose either is to live a lie, but it's a rare person who relishes going against the flow, questioning the establishment, or speaking the truth when it is unpopular or misunderstood.

Galatians 5:1 (NIV) says, "It is for freedom that Christ has set us free." We belong to God, body and soul. We have been freed from the bondage of human opinion and religious legalism. We are free to follow Christ without fear. We are held in the palm of His hand.

I praise You, Lord, for the freedom You give. Help me to live every hour emboldened by that truth.

Set Free from Bondage

But Jesus shot back, "You frauds! Each Sabbath
every one of you regularly unties your cow or
donkey from its stall, leads it out for water, and thinks
nothing of it. So why isn't it all right for me to untie
this daughter of Abraham and lead her from the stall
where Satan has had her tied these eighteen years?"

LUKE 13:15–16 MSG

As Jesus was teaching in the meeting place on the
Sabbath, he saw a woman there who was so bent
over with a disability that she could not even look up.
She had been this way for eighteen years. He called
her over and spoke the words, "Woman, you are
free." She immediately stood straight in response to
the word of her Creator. Just as He calmed the wind
and waves, He now spoke to her body, and finally
she was able to lift her head. Imagine her elation.
The thrill, the release, the rush, the excitement—

Jesus had set her free from the bondage her body had held her in for so long. She glorified Him in that moment with her every cell.

You would think that everyone around her would be celebrating with her, but the ruler of the synagogue was angry because Jesus had healed her on the Sabbath. He accused Jesus of breaking the Sabbath rules about work. Jesus goes straight to the irony and hypocrisy of the accusation. These men freed their animals from their stalls on the Sabbath because that is what they needed; He freed this woman because she needed Him. In that instant, He put to shame His accusers; they had no comeback.

There will always be onlookers watching the kingdom of God unfold who want to criticize, to bind, to judge, and to minimize. Celebrate what Jesus did for this woman and does for each of us. He calls to us, lifts up our heads, frees us, and defends us against our accusers.

Thank You for delivering me from all the stalls that have held me in, for lifting up my head, and sending Jesus to set me free.

On Our Side

Out of my distress I called on the LORD; the LORD
answered me and set me free. The LORD is on
my side; I will not fear. What can man do to me?
PSALM 118:5–6 ESV

We experience fears of all kinds, but one of our chief fears is other people. We want others' approval. We want to please our friends, family, and coworkers. We fear not being or doing enough in the eyes of other people. We fear being left behind or not being successful. We fear not being treated fairly by others. We fear being ostracized. We fear being under the authority of people we don't agree with. We fear not being in power or having control over our own lives. Whether we want to admit it or not, we fear what people can do to us.

The psalmist reminds us that God is on our side. God, our Father, whose ear is always attuned to the cry of His child, is right next to us. He hears the call of His distressed, frightened children. We cannot conquer fear by ourselves, and we cannot conquer all our fears in a onetime experience or in one morning's prayer. But daily we can call to God, our Father. Whatever has put us in distress that day, whatever fear crops up to hold us in bondage, that hour we can cry out to God in prayer to deliver us.

To live in fear is to live in bondage. Only God can free us. Call out to Him when fear attacks. He is on your side. He will set you free.

Thank You, Father in heaven,
that You will set me free from
fear every time I call out to You.

Jesus the Victor

*All that passing laws against sin did was
produce more lawbreakers. But sin didn't,
and doesn't, have a chance in competition
with the aggressive forgiveness we call grace.*
ROMANS 5:20–21 MSG

There is a war going on around us every day. It is
between good and evil, freedom and bondage, sin
and forgiveness. The battle between spirit and flesh,
life and death, fatigues us. We are affected by this
battle whether we acknowledge its reality or not.

We are bombarded constantly with messages
from our culture to turn to false gods of beauty,
power, and control, or money and security. We're
tempted to be discouraged when we don't measure
up to the images of women in the media, or even
real ones around us. We are frustrated when we
can't get others to cooperate with the agendas we

set. We are depressed when we don't have all that we want. Sometimes we wallow in false guilt over prideful expectations we set for ourselves yet fail to meet.

But there's good news: in the battle for your body and soul, Jesus is the victor, more powerful than any sin you've been enslaved to or any temptation nagging you. His forgiveness overcomes all sin. His grace hunts you down and draws you away from sin and toward his love and mercy. Thank Him today for conquering all sin—past, present, and future.

Lord Christ, Your forgiveness and
Your grace are greater than anything
in my life. Help me to rest in that truth.

Free to Fail

For a righteous man may fall seven times and rise again, but the wicked shall fall by calamity.

PROVERBS 24:16 NKJV

John 8:36 (NIV) says, "'If the Son sets you free, you will be free indeed.'" We are free—from sin, from fear, from the bondage of the law, from the expectations of others, and from the approval of others. We are even free to fail. Righteous men fall; they fall over and over. But they are forgiven and by God's grace get up and move toward Christ again and again. Jesus was lifted up on a cross for our failures. He died for our sins, our imperfections, our flaws, and our inability to conquer our own temptations and desires. We will fall. We will fail. To expect otherwise is to be filled with pride.

We need the Spirit constantly. Only the particulars of what we need in the moment change. One day it's wisdom; another day, longsuffering. We fail at patience. We fail at kindness. We fail at compassion, at self-control, at holding our tongues. We fail at managing our money or our time. We fail at giving.

But even as we fall, we can see God's grace. We learn to accept our neediness, our frailty, and our humanity. Our pride diminishes with repeated failure. Our compassion for others grows as we face our own failures.

Don't go seeking failure; but when it comes, allow it to be an experience of learning more grace. Praise God for His faithfulness in setting us free— free even to fail.

Father, by Your grace I am forgiven and free. Failure does not separate me from Your love. Thank You.

Free to Follow Christ

*I will run in the way of your commandments
when you enlarge my heart!*
PSALM 119:32 ESV

Being a bighearted person or a freehanded host does not come naturally. We come into the world crying to have our wants and needs satisfied; and for some people, little changes as they age. Generosity and other-centeredness have to be cultivated; they are a response to what we see and experience.

When Jesus enters our lives, He begins to enlarge our hearts. He frees us from the burden of guilt over our sin and the burden of obsessing over ourselves. Only then, when we have been forgiven, can we begin to give generously to others. Because Jesus forgives us, we are free to forgive others. Because He provides for us, we are free to provide for others. Because He gently leads us, we are gentle with those we lead. The world opens to us. Emotional reactions to others become possible for us because Jesus is alive in our hearts, enlarging our capacity to love by His liberating love. This is what it means to be set free—free to love, free to follow Christ, free to run in the way of His commandments.

---

*Thank You, Christ Jesus, for freeing
me from the bondage of sin and self.
Continue to enlarge my heart toward others.*

His Word Liberates

That set everyone back on their heels, whispering and wondering, "What's going on here? Someone whose words make things happen? Someone who orders demonic spirits to get out and they go?" Jesus was the talk of the town.

LUKE 4:36–37 MSG

I'm going to tell Mom," one sibling yells to another. "Get in the game," a coach yells to a player. "You're hired (or fired)," the boss says. We all know that person who speaks and things get done. The power of a word or two from certain people can change the course of a life, a business, an institution, an economy, or a nation.

The power of the word is carried in the authority of the one who speaks it. Jesus' words in Luke 4 are powerful. He ordered demons out of a man and healed a sick woman by the power of His spoken word. He has power over evil, illness, and even death. He is the Word of God. He was with God in creation when, by the words spoken, a world came into existence.

Jesus' words are like no other. Power resides in them. What does He say? Read the scripture. Follow Him through the Gospels. Pray for faith to believe. Listen to His Spirit speak. His Word makes things happen. His Word gives life. His word liberates us. Praise God today that by His Word we are set free to follow Him.

Thank You, Lord, for the power of Your Word to set free those whom You love. Give me faith to believe Your Word.

Vigilant Angels

For he will command his angels concerning you to guard you in all your ways. On their hands they will bear you up, lest you strike your foot against a stone.
PSALM 91:11–12 ESV

Freedom is won for a nation when soldiers go to battle and fight for it. Freedom is preserved when they stay on duty and guard against attack. When a country or a city is well patrolled, those who live in it can work, play, and sleep in peace, knowing guards standing watch are protecting them day and night.

Women wrestle with many fears: change that the future brings, being alone in old age, losing a child, failing health, or losing a relationship. Yet we have a loving Father who has commanded angels to keep us from falling. We can be free from fear by remembering who God is and what He has done.

God has commanded His heavenly hosts, the

angels, to guard His people. They are constantly vigilant, though we rarely think of them, doing the bidding of Almighty God. Throughout the scriptures, angels are sent to deliver messages, and often they begin with the words, "Do not fear."

_____

God, I'm so grateful for the ministering angels whom You've sent to protect me. Make me more attentive to Your protection over my life.

Scripture Fulfilled

Unrolling the scroll, he found the place where it was written, "God's Spirit is on me; he's chosen me to preach the Message of good news to the poor, sent me to announce pardon to prisoners and recovery of sight to the blind, to set the burdened and battered free, to announce, 'This is God's year to act!'" He rolled up the scroll, handed it back to the assistant, and sat down. Every eye in the place was on him, intent. Then he started in, "You've just heard Scripture make history. It came true just now in this place."

LUKE 4:17–21 MSG

Imagine being in the synagogue that day when Jesus read those words from Isaiah. Here He was claiming to be the very one Isaiah had prophesied. The scripture was being fulfilled before their very eyes. He chose this passage, one proclaiming that He will bring good news and pardon prisoners, that

He will give sight to the blind and free the burdened and the battered. That same Jesus still stands today, revealing Himself likewise to us.

What prison are you in? What part of life do you feel trapped in with no means of escape? In what areas do you desperately want freedom but can't seem to find it on your own? Are there things you can't see? Is there darkness in your life? Think of the burdens you carry, and imagine Jesus taking them from you and carrying them Himself.

Jesus came to save us, to set us free. Our physical circumstances may or may not change, but when He comes into our lives, His presence opens that prison. He carries our burdens for us. His light dissipates the darkness that blinds us.

---

*Jesus, You came into this world
and You saved my life.
Thank You.*

Anchored to Jesus

Jesus instructed him, "Don't talk about this all over town. Just quietly present your healed self to the priest, along with the offering ordered by Moses. Your cleansed and obedient life, not your words, will bear witness to what I have done."

LUKE 5:14 MSG

Freedom manifests itself in action.

What if someone filmed you for a day? What did you do? What did you talk about at the office or on the phone to your friends? Would your life match what you say you believe is true about Jesus?

Freedom is not being untied, like a boat cast out on a reckless sea. Freedom is being anchored to Jesus, so sure of your security that the waves and the winds don't matter. Freedom is not calm seas but no fear of the seas. To be fearful is to live in bondage. Whether we are afraid someone will get ahead of us or that someone has more influence or is more popular, or afraid to defend ourselves when accused, when we are afraid we are not free. Jesus saved us to be free. Galatians 5:1 says it was for freedom that Christ set us free. When our days are spent living for others' approval, stepping on people to get to the top, tearing others down with gossip and slander, or worrying about the future, we should stop and reflect on what Jesus has done for us.

Praise God that He has cleansed you and set you free, that your life can be a psalm of praise to His greatness.

Help me remember, Lord Jesus,
that my freedom in this world is
because I am anchored to You.

*W*hen you come to knowing God, the initiative lies on His side. If He does not show Himself, nothing you can do will enable you to find Him.

—C. S. Lewis

His Revelation

Light for the Eyes

*"No one lights a lamp, then hides it in a drawer.
It's put on a lamp stand so those entering the room
have light to see where they're going. Your eye is a
lamp, lighting up your whole body. If you live wide-
eyed in wonder and belief, your body fills up with light.
If you live squinty-eyed in greed and distrust, your
body is a dank cellar. Keep your eyes open, your lamp
burning, so you don't get musty and murky. Keep your
life as well-lighted as your best-lighted room."*

LUKE 11:36 MSG

Eyes are like lamps. They illuminate the world before
us. The condition of our eyes determines our perspective or view of the people and circumstances
around us. How do we see the world? Do we live
wide-eyed and in wonder as the scripture says, or do
we shut out light by being greedy and distrustful?
There's an old English proverb: "The eyes are the

window to the soul." A window lets light in and enables us to see the larger outside world. The shape and size of the window, whether it is dirty or clean, color what we see outside.

Jesus tells us to look wide-eyed and in wonder, that is, to look long, to gaze, to stare, think, notice, reflect on, and pay attention to the world around us, finding beauty and meaning in everything. And He cautions us against a squinty-eyed life. Luke 12:15 (MSG) says, "Take care! Protect yourself against the least bit of greed. Life is not defined by what you have, even when you have a lot." Greed and distrust shut out light. Think of a cellar. When light is shut out, mold, rot, and ruin are rampant. Greed and distrust are the warning signs. When they surface in our lives, we need to confess them and ask for help.

Thank You, God, for the light You give.
I want to be wide-eyed, to let more light
in and to see the world the way You see it.

Wisdom

*So teach us to number our days
that we may get a heart of wisdom.*
Psalm 90:12 esv

When something special is on our calendars, we tend to count the days. We eagerly anticipate a wedding date, the arrival of a baby, a long-awaited vacation, or a reunion with family members. Excitement builds as the date nears, and each day in between seems to move slowly. Counting down the days is fun.

Numbering the days until we die, however, is not something we ordinarily think about. But God's Word tells us to do this because in doing so we will gain wisdom. How so? When we contemplate the brevity of life or the fact that sooner or later our lives on earth do come to an end, we cannot help but reflect on our relationship to God and on who and what is important in our lives. When we think like this, we tend to reorder priorities, to set things right with other people, and to let go of the petty and shallow things in life and focus on what matters. This reflection and repentance opens the door to wisdom. Ecclesiastes 8:1 says wisdom brightens a man's face, and Proverbs 24:14 says that wisdom is sweet to our souls.

Thank You, Lord, for the gift of wisdom. Help me think rightly about time, being reflective and repentant so that wisdom will be mine.

God's Generous Revelation

Have you ever come on anything quite like this extravagant generosity of God, this deep, deep wisdom? It's way over our heads. We'll never figure it out. Is there anyone around who can explain God? Anyone smart enough to tell him what to do? Anyone who has done him such a huge favor that God has to ask his advice? Everything comes from him; everything happens through him; everything ends up in him. Always glory! Always praise! Yes. Yes. Yes.

ROMANS 11:33 –36 MSG

It's hard to understand how the creator God of the universe can also be our personal Savior and call us friends. No matter how many sermons we hear, Bible studies we attend, or how much theology we read, we really cannot grasp His being both a personal Lord and constant companion as well as the majestic, sovereign King of the universe. We tend to stand in awe of that awesome God "out there" who made it all and controls it all, but we forget to draw near with the smallest concerns of our day-to-day lives. Or we view Him as close and personal, talking to Him about all that concerns us, but then we slip into thinking He is so like us that we limit our view of His power and grandeur. He is both as close as our breath and as expansive as the farthest galaxy. He cares about every detail that concerns us, and yet He controls the movements of the planets and the tides. Part of coming to know Him is learning to live with this mystery, accepting that our view of Him will always be skewed and incomplete. He knows that too, and He promises that one day we will see Him as He is.

Today, pause to think about how you view Him right now. Is He "out there" but too distant? Do you feel close to Him, but your view of Him is too low? Ask God to open your eyes to more. Thank Him for His faithfulness to reveal Himself.

Thank You, heavenly Father,
for revealing Yourself to me.

Holy Spirit Help

*Now we have received not the spirit of the world,
but the Spirit who is from God, that we might
understand the things freely given us by God.
And we impart this in words not taught by human
wisdom but taught by the Spirit, interpreting
spiritual truths to those who are spiritual.*

1 CORINTHIANS 2:12–13 ESV

We have been given wisdom whether we know it or not. In one sense, we could say we are wiser than we know. That sense is the gift we have been given by the Holy Spirit. His dwelling in us allows us to interpret spiritual truths and to help one another in our daily lives. God has freely given us life in Christ and desires that we understand all that is ours in that new identity.

The problem we have is that we primarily rely on our own human wisdom and knowledge. We haven't trained ourselves to listen to the Spirit's voice. We don't know the Word of God well enough to let it be of optimum use in our lives. We tend to function in the strength of our own personalities and follow paths that seem logical to us. But the realm of the Spirit is not always logical, and the wisdom He gives us doesn't always look like a smart thing to do or say by the world's standards. Die in order to live. Give instead of get. Lay down your life. Take up your cross. The very things that sound foolish are wise when the Spirit opens our eyes.

I praise You, Father, for giving me the wisdom of the Holy Spirit. Forgive me for neglecting this gift and trying to rely on my own self-sufficiency.

Divine Display

Open your eyes and there it is! By taking a long and thoughtful look at what God has created, people have always been able to see what their eyes as such can't see: eternal power, for instance, and the mystery of his divine being.

ROMANS 1:19–20 MSG

See the clarity of a blue autumn sky on a chilly morning. Smell the damp, rotting leaves that will become next year's food for the trees. Feel the winds that bring rain on a summer afternoon. Watch the mother robin sitting on her eggs. Gaze at her eating red berries growing on a nearby bush. Listen to the ocean continually lapping the shore. Admire the agility of the squirrels jumping from limb to limb. Refresh yourself in the shade of a water oak. Smell the skin of a newborn infant.

Eternal power and the mystery of the divine are

on display constantly. God does not hide Himself. He is right before our eyes. Every facet of creation—motion, rhythm, color, shape, or texture—displays something of His majestic being. He is the creator of all; He has revealed Himself in bits of truth throughout all creation. We only have to look, to ask for eyes to see and then hearts to worship the sovereign King and divine Architect behind it all.

The beauty all around me speaks of You. Help me to be attentive to Your constant revelation.

Stories of Jesus

*With many stories like these, he presented
his message to them, fitting the stories to their
experience and maturity. He was never without
a story when he spoke. When he was alone
with his disciples, he went over everything,
sorting out the tangles, untying the knots.*

MARK 4:33–34 MSG

Jesus used story as a primary teaching tool with his disciples and with the crowds that came to hear Him. He used the tangible things of the world that His listeners knew to illustrate the kingdom of God to them. Acorns, talents, seeds, weeds, sheep, lamps, doors, judges, wineskins, coins—all the stuff of ordinary life became subjects of His stories.

Look around. He is still doing this every day for you. Reflect on what He places before your eyes. What is the meaning in what you see? What are the stories you are currently living in? Think of the memorable events in your past, and thank God for them. Reflect on what you learned in those stories. Rehearse those lessons and share them with others.

Thank God today for our powers of observation, analogies, metaphors, and illustrations—all the ways He teaches through stories.

Almighty God, thank You for making Yourself known to me. Enable me to see You in all things.

Who Is He?

Awake now, he told the wind to pipe down and said to the sea, "Quiet! Settle down!" The wind ran out of breath; the sea became smooth as glass. Jesus reprimanded the disciples: "Why are you such cowards? Don't you have any faith at all?" They were in absolute awe, staggered. "Who is this, anyway?" they asked. "Wind and sea at his beck and call!"

MARK 4:39–41 MSG

He spoke, and the sea was stilled and the wind stopped. The question His disciples asked, "Who is this?" is one that will come to us too on our spiritual journeys. The more we come to know God, the more we realize how little we know. He is beyond our comprehension, eternal, and mysterious. We will only experience slivers and rays of His glorious light. We know bits and pieces. "We see in a mirror dimly" (1 Corinthians 13:12 ESV).

Part of the journey is becoming comfortable with this question: "Who is this?" If we are seeing the Holy Spirit's activity in our lives, we will continually be surprised. Our ideas of God will broaden and deepen. We will become confident that we are safe and loved by Him, even as we are less able to define Him. We may even have times of fear and confusion, just as the disciples did. But with every storm that blows up in our lives, with every tumultuous trial we face, we know He has all power and authority, even as we find ourselves awed and asking, "Who is He?" Thank God today for His infinite power and glory and beauty.

Lord, may I continually be awed by Your presence and Your work in my life and the world around me. Help me not to be afraid of the mystery but rather to worship You.

Christ in Us

"Listen carefully to what I am saying—and be wary of the shrewd advice that tells you how to get ahead in the world on your own. Giving, not getting, is the way. Generosity begets generosity. Stinginess impoverishes."

MARK 4:24–25 MSG

Giving, Jesus says, is the way to get ahead in the world. Like most things Jesus said, this idea runs counter to the world's wisdom. The world teaches us to protect ourselves, take the credit, save our time, trust very few, and amass all we can. Jesus says living that way will impoverish us; we should give instead. Give time, give credit, give trust, and give wealth.

Giving diminishes self, which enlarges Christ in us. Giving frees us from hoarding, from fear of want, and exercises our trust in God's provision for the future. Giving reflects God's generosity toward us and passes it on to others. Giving feels good and brings rewards we cannot imagine until we do it. Jesus knows the joy in it for us; that's why He tells us to do it.

What do we have that we can share—money, food, clothing, time? What about encouragement, credit for a job well done, respect, a smile, a compliment, trust, the truth, a listening ear, spending time with someone?

Ask God to open your eyes to His generous Spirit so that we may become generous. Look for creative ways to step into this freedom He offers by giving more.

Thank You for giving generously to me.
Help me to become more like
You in giving to others.

Resistance as Invitation

Your testimonies are wonderful; therefore my soul keeps them. The unfolding of your words gives light; it imparts understanding to the simple.
PSALM 119:129–130 ESV

You walk by your Bible on an end table and think about sitting down to read. But another task awaits you. The to-do list always beckons. *I'll get to it in a few minutes,* you think. But the few minutes turn into hours, and then it's bedtime or time to go to work. A day or two goes by and you notice an inner resistance to the sight of the Bible on the table—as if something inside you is avoiding sitting still with that book.

Finally you decide to stop and read. You experience the refreshment of the Psalms, the reminder of God's saving, healing, forgiving love. The love, the presence, the goodness of God all flood your mind, just from a verse or two. You start talking to God about the upcoming day, your worries, problems, and needs. Suddenly you feel free, open, peaceful, and confident to face the day, knowing you're not alone.

Why do we resist being fed by God's Word? This is the war between our flesh and His Spirit. Our egos will always fight for control, not wanting to surrender to God and experience His presence. What if we could learn to see our resistance as an invitation? When the internal conversation starts—*I don't have enough time; I'll pray later; I'll read the Word another day*—that mind chatter is God's invitation to us. He is beckoning, and our egos fight back.

Thank You for drawing me to Yourself, even when I don't recognize it. Help me see my own resistance as an invitation to the very thing I need.

*N*o child of God sins to that degree as to make himself incapable of forgiveness.

—JOHN BUNYAN

His Forgiveness

Liberated

Let it be known to you therefore, brothers, that through this man forgiveness of sins is proclaimed to you, and by him everyone who believes is freed from everything from which you could not be freed by the law of Moses.

ACTS 13:38–39 ESV

In the courtroom, the judge, not the law, sets a man free. The law is only a written code. It serves as a standard of behavior, but is has no power to declare a man guilty or innocent. The power resides with a person. The judge must speak. A ruling must be given for an accused man to walk away free.

In times of war, when prisoners are held, someone has to go unlock the gates. They are not free when the cease-fire is signed; they are free when the rescuing soldiers pour through those gates and take them outside the fences.

Jesus is the judge who gives the verdict. Jesus is the liberating warrior. When He went to the cross and died for our sins, He declared us not guilty. When He walked out of that tomb, having conquered death, He released our bonds. His life, death, and resurrection were for us. Ephesians 1:7 says we have redemption through His blood. Sin held us as slaves, but God has bought us back with the blood of Christ.

Christ Jesus, Son of the living God, thank You for giving Your life for mine. Thank You for forgiving my sins and declaring me innocent. Show me how to live my life of freedom to honor You.

Forgetting Sin

"This is the brand-new covenant that I will make with Israel when the time comes. I will put my law within them—write it on their hearts!—and be their God. And they will be my people. They will no longer go around setting up schools to teach each other about God. They'll know me firsthand, the dull and the bright, the smart and the slow. I'll wipe the slate clean for each of them. I'll forget they ever sinned!" God's Decree.

JEREMIAH 31:33–34 MSG

Think about what it's like to not remember. To truly forget is usually frustrating for us. We can't remember someone's name. We realize the details of a favorite childhood memory have now become fuzzy. Rarely is forgetting a good thing, though occasionally we are glad we have forgotten. The physical pain of childbirth fades somewhat. The piercing heartache of grief dulls, though never goes away completely. We find we can finally talk about a painful emotional experience without tears or anger rising in our throats.

Even when we want to forget pain, the best we can do is hope for a dulled memory. But God can choose, and He does choose, to completely forget our sin. Truthfully, we cannot really comprehend how God can forget our sin. Forgetting seems contrary to an eternal and everlasting being; yet by His own will He erases the memory of our sin.

Think of the joy and the beauty and the power in that—choosing to forget that you have been wronged, completely wiping the scene from memory. Thank God today for His power to willfully forget our sin.

Thank You, Father, that because of Jesus,
You have willingly forgotten my sin.

God's Specialty

*Where is the god who can compare with you—
wiping the slate clean of guilt, turning a blind
eye, a deaf ear, to the past sins of your purged
and precious people? You don't nurse your anger
and don't stay angry long, for mercy is your
specialty. That's what you love most.*
MICAH 7:18–19 MSG

Some women are talented at arranging flowers or gardening. Others sew beautiful garments or make crafts, while some have that special dish that they can make taste better than anyone else's. We all have our specialties. God also has a specialty. It's mercy. He shows it endlessly, willfully, and to extents that we cannot comprehend or exercise ourselves. He loves to show mercy. He loves to forgive us, though we never deserve it.

A blind eye cannot see at all. A deaf ear cannot

hear. The accusations we hurl at ourselves or listen to from the enemy, long after God has forgiven us, are unseen and unheard by God. He is not playing the scene of our sin over and over in His mind like we do, endlessly and pointlessly going over the broken past. He willfully chooses to forget, completely. Praise Him today for His faithful mercy, which continues daily in your life.

Merciful God, I cannot comprehend Your goodness, but help me to accept by faith Your endless mercy and forgiveness.

Restored by God

Restore us, O God; let your
face shine, that we may be saved!
<small>PSALM 80:3 ESV</small>

For a few years, the blue screen with the blinking cursor was bad news. Now the "black screen of death," as some call it, haunts those who work on computers. Backing up to cloud servers or copying to jump drives is essential in today's workplaces—you never know when or if a computer might crash. You only have to experience a crash once to know the frustration of losing work or important data, pictures, and documents. Finding someone who can restore the computer, who can take it back to its original settings and recover all that was lost, is a moment of sweet relief.

Multiply that relief by tens of thousands as you think about how God restores us. Over and over, through the saving work of Christ, He restores us into fellowship with Him. He repeatedly forgives our sins. He constantly returns our joy. He continually provides His presence. When we call on Him in our distress, when we cry out in repentance, He is always willing and able to restore us, to set things back just as they were, in the moment He redeemed us.

Praise God that His face always shines on us, that there is never a moment He will not restore us to fellowship with Him.

Gracious God, Your redeeming love
is constantly restoring me. Help me
to remember that and celebrate.

God's Gentle Question

But it displeased Jonah exceedingly, and he was angry. And he prayed to the LORD and said, "O LORD, is not this what I said when I was yet in my country? That is why I made haste to flee to Tarshish; for I knew that you are a gracious God and merciful, slow to anger and abounding in steadfast love, and relenting from disaster. Therefore now, O LORD, please take my life from me, for it is better for me to die than to live." And the LORD said, "Do you do well to be angry?"

JONAH 4:1–4 ESV

Jonah had fled God's call. He had run the other way when God wanted to send him to the people of Nineveh. His remarkable experience in the belly of a whale had taught him the futility of running from God. His life had been spared miraculously, and he finally went on to Nineveh to proclaim God's Word. Amazingly, he becomes angry when God relents and does not punish the people of Nineveh once they repent.

Is it really so hard to believe though? Jonah, representative of prideful, self-righteous human nature, has quickly forgotten how he ran from God. Once he turned and obeyed God by going to preach to the people of Nineveh, he wanted to see them punished. He wanted justice, not mercy.

God gently nudges him with a probing question: "Do you do well to be angry?" Many times anger is rooted in pride, and this question teases it out of us. We didn't get our way; things didn't work out according to our agenda; someone got away with something they shouldn't have. Is pride or self-righteousness at the root of our anger? Are we envious of God's grace in another's life because we have forgotten His mercy and grace to us?

Thank Him for His gentle question: "Do you do well to be angry?"

I praise You, Father, for Your faithfulness
to continually root out sin in my life
and draw me back to You.

No Record

*If you, LORD, kept a record of sins, Lord, who could
stand? But with you there is forgiveness, so that
we can, with reverence, serve you.*

PSALM 130:3–4 NIV

Our society keeps records. We record who is born,
who can vote, who can drive, who owns a home, who is
registered for the draft, who gets married, divorced,
and dies. We generate a receipt for every purchase
made. We continue to develop technology with the
capacity to store more and more information.

But the Lord does not keep a record of sin. We
read right over the psalmist's words because we
cannot comprehend that. What in our lives is not
recorded? With a record of every piece of electronic
communication and the potential that anyone with
a phone might be making a video, is it possible to
grasp that there is not a record of our sin?

Meditate on the truth that the Lord does not keep a record of sin. It is gone. He does not remember it. He dealt with it on Calvary, and He remembers it no more. Ask God for help to believe a promise that's so foreign to our current culture. He offers us complete forgiveness. Our sin is erased. He keeps no record. Stand in awe of such grace and mercy. Celebrate that you stand cleared before Him. Thank Him for such love.

Father God, I am awed that
You keep no record of my sin.
Give me faith to live out this truth.

Spirit's Light

*Blessed is the man against whom
the LORD counts no iniquity, and in
whose spirit there is no deceit.*

PSALM 32:2 ESV

Blessed means "happy." The forgiven man is happy. He accepts the finished work of Jesus on the cross and knows his sins are forgiven. He's happy because he is not trying to earn his way to heaven by good works, and he is not laden with false guilt.

Beyond that though is the inner joy that comes with knowing your heart is clean by the practice of confession. It's one thing to know you are forgiven intellectually—it's another to experience the healing cleansing of confession.

Too often we are content to mentally assent to being forgiven. We know the sins of our past are gone according to God, and that is good news enough. But we're shortchanging ourselves when we don't take the extra step of asking God's Spirit to probe our hearts, to show us if there is anything we are hiding from ourselves. We are masters of self-deception and rationalization. Oftentimes depressed feelings or frustration and anger can be attributed to things we are holding on to in our hearts but will not admit to our heads—the idols, the secrets, the anger, or the pride. Only the Spirit can show us when and how we deceive ourselves. The abundant joy that Christ died to give us comes when we allow the Spirit to shine light into our hearts, showing us the dark places, so we can confess, let go, and receive His peace and comfort.

---

*Holy Spirit, thank You for shining light into
my heart and showing me my deception.
Fill me with abundant joy in the grace of Christ.*

Pleasing Sacrifices

The sacrifices of God are a broken spirit:
a broken and a contrite heart,
O God, thou wilt not despise.
PSALM 51:17 KJV

Though we should be relieved that God does not require us to check a list of commandments and good works or to sacrifice livestock as we enter the temple, it might be easier to do those things than to offer the sacrifice that most pleases Him. A broken heart and a contrite spirit are not things we can readily produce in ourselves. In fact, we cannot produce them at all. God must work in us to bring us to repentance.

Our human nature will want to remain emotionally comfortable—and that is not a contrite spirit. Everything in us resists brokenness. No one likes to feel heartache. We have hundreds of ways to mask the pain of brokenness, to avoid facing our own messes. Feeling good is a modern-day idol; facing your own sin is discouraged at every turn. But this is what pleases God.

How do we offer Him the sacrifice that pleases Him? We step back and start with a prayer for mercy—confessing that we don't have broken hearts and we don't feel sorry for our sins, and we don't really have a willingness to change. Then we ask for a willingness to be open rather than resistant, for a teachable spirit, for an ear to hear and agree with what the Spirit of God is saying.

Thank You, God, for starting right where I am.
I only have to bring You myself, in whatever state
I am in, and You help me to begin again.

Reality of the Heart

"The good person out of the good treasure of his heart produces good, and the evil person out of his evil treasure produces evil, for out of the abundance of the heart his mouth speaks."

LUKE 6:45 ESV

Reality TV, regardless of how "real" it actually is, is probably with us to stay. The popularity of the genre is attributed to our desire for attention and fame, even in the ordinariness of daily life. The most tragic and comic moments are often captured in one-liners—the unrehearsed things the characters say. What is in our hearts comes out eventually in what we say.

Some people always seem to turn to criticizing or gossiping about other people. Others talk only about themselves. There's the victim, the pessimist, and the cynic, who can never find the good in other people or things. Then there's the one who praises and encourages others or brings peace to a conflict—the voice of hope, steadfastness, support, and acceptance.

What if a reality TV camera followed us around for a day and recorded every conversation, including the looks in our eyes and the nuances of our body language? The speech from our lips is like a thermometer for our hearts. How would it read?

Pray that God would create in you a clean heart and let no unwholesome thing come out of your mouth. Remember 1 John 1:9 (NIV): "If we confess our sins, he is faithful and just and will forgive us our sins and purify us from all unrighteousness."

Lord, thank You for Your faithfulness to forgive my sins and to make me more like You. Make me a person of gracious speech for the sake of Your kingdom.

Clean and New

*"Come now, let us reason together,
says the LORD: though your sins are like scarlet,
they shall be as white as snow; though they are
red like crimson, they shall become like wool."*

ISAIAH 1:18 ESV

Most women despise doing laundry. It's just a necessary fact of life. Dirty clothes will always be with us. The sheets continually have to be changed. Someone has to take the towels from the dryer and fold them again. The task of pretreating stains is no fun, as there is usually little hope of success. Despite the various products and techniques for stain removal, many spots don't quite come out. The rug or the sofa cushion may always have that faint circle from a spill. Ink is nearly impossible to get out of a garment. But occasionally you experience a moment of joy when that ketchup stain, the one that should have ruined your favorite white blouse, actually does come out.

Picture your soul as a fresh, crisp white shirt marred with a black ink spill. Hopeless, if you are the laundress. Imagine if you could actually get the ink out and restore that shirt to its original beauty. That is what God has done. The ink of sin is gone, the blackness of guilt is washed out, and you are restored.

God does not remember the stain. He does not remind us of the work it took to get it out. He says our sins are to Him as pure white snow and undyed wool. He has forgotten that they ever marred us. Celebrate the newness of your life in Christ.

Thank You, God, for forgiving me. Help me to remember that though I may never forget my sins, You have chosen to forget them.

Looking for More Encouragement for Your Heart?

Worry Less, Pray More

This purposeful devotional guide features 180 readings and prayers designed to help alleviate your worries as you learn to live in the peace of the Almighty God, who offers calm for your anxiety-filled soul.

Paperback / 978-1-68322-861-5 / $4.99

Too Blessed to be Stressed: 3-Minute Devotions for Women

You'll find the spiritual pick-me-up you need in *Too Blessed to Be Stressed: 3-Minute Devotions for Women*. 180 uplifting readings from bestselling author Debora M. Coty pack a powerful dose of inspiration, encouragement, humor, and faith into just-right-sized readings for your busy schedule.

Paperback / 978-1-63409-569-3 / $4.99